D1114545

SLEEPY PRINCESS
IN THE DEMON CASTLE

10

STORY & ART BY

KAGIJI KUMANOMATA

NIGHTS

118th Night: You Don't Know Anything

LAST NIGHT...
...I COULDN'T STAND THE SUSPENSE ANYMORE, SO I FINALLY DECIDED TO ASK THE PRINCESS...
PRINCESS!

PRINCESS... DO YOU HAVE ANY INTENTION OF ANNIHILATING THE DEMONS...?
HUH?
YOU'VE BEEN A HOSTAGE AT THE DEMON CASTLE FOR QUITE SOME TIME NOW.
...
AND I AM A GRIMOIRE. WHICH MEANS... IF YOU MAKE PROPER USE OF ME, YOU ARE CAPABLE OF DESTROYING THE DEMONS. WHERE IS THE HATRED IN YOUR HEART FOR YOUR DEMON CAPTORS?!
...
...

ANY-HOO... COULD YOU OPEN TO YOUR PAGE ON HOW TO MAKE BEDDING?
YOU CERTAINLY ARE FOND OF THAT PAGE...

ROLL
ROLL
VERY WELL...
FROM THIS DAY FORTH, I WILL RELINQUISH ANY EXPECTATIONS OF THE PRINCESS.

OF COURSE, I AM GRATEFUL TO HER FOR BREAKING MY SEAL.
I SUPPOSE IT WAS WRONG OF ME TO EVER EXPECT THE PRINCESS, A MERE HOSTAGE, TO BE THE SOURCE OF THE DEMONS' DOWNFALL...
QUEST USE ONLY
ROLL
ROLL

GOODBYE, PRINCESS! TODAY IS THE DAY I...
...DEPART FROM THE DEMON CASTLE!
Close-up
?
Ha ha ha
THIS IS SO HEAVY.
QUEST
QUEST USE ONLY

118th Night: You Don't Know Anything

I DON'T GET IT THOUGH... THE ONLY THING SHE HAS USED ME TO DESTROY WERE THE BEE-BEE DEMONS.
I'm scared of bees!
OTHER THAN THAT, SHE SPENDS ALL HER TIME SLEEPING OR PLAYING.
AND I AM THE ONLY WEAPON AT THE PRINCESS'S DISPOSAL.
I'm sleepy!
I want to use my MP to...
...fight the nudist!
Actually, I need a nap.
The princess Alazif knows
THIS PRINCESS LACKS THE FORTITUDE TO ERADICATE DEMONKIND.

I SHALL JOIN THE HERO WHO WILL MAKE BETTER USE OF ME!
THE HERO I HAVE YET TO MEET
rolll
rolll
I CAN ONLY OBSERVE HER WHEN MY PAGES ARE OPEN, BUT IT'S CLEAR THAT THE PRINCESS IS NOTHING MORE THAN A SLIGHTLY PECULIAR HOSTAGE.
THIS WILL BE A LONG JOURNEY ...
... BUT THE PRINCESS CAN WAIT SAFELY HERE IN CAPTIVITY.
UEST USE ON

CH

OOPS ...
I MIS-TOOK IT FOR ...
FWABA

VWIP
...

MISTOOK IT FOR WHAT?!
A Ghost Shroud

AND WHAT ARE THOSE SCISSORS FOR?!
*Unbelievable as it may seem, Alazif has never seen the princess wielding her scissors.
Aiiee
The princess usually keeps the grimoire shut.

W-WELL, I KNOW SHE OFTEN POPS OUT OF HER CELL...
roll
roll
B-BUT THIS DEMON PAID HER VIOLENT BEHAVIOR NO MIND... THIS DOESN'T MAKE SENSE!
M-MAYBE I JUST IMAGINED IT ALL...
KLANG

KLANG KLANG KLANG KLANG KLANG
ARRRGH!
WHAT IS SHE UP TO ...?!

EH?! THE TREASURE CHEST? WHAT IS SHE DOING TO IT?
KLANG KLANG KLANG KLANG
HEY! WHY ISN'T THIS DEMON TAKING ANY NOTICE OF HER STRANGE BEHAVIOR?!

AWW... SHE'S SO LIVELY!
"LIVELY" ISN'T THE WORD!

H-HEY, DEMON!
HUH? Who are you?
OVER THERE! WHAT IS THE PRINCESS DOING?!
UM...
USING A DEMON AS A BLACK-JACK TO DESTROY THE TREASURE CHEST, I GUESS.
AARRRGH!
KLANG
KLANG
KLANG
KLANG
KLANG
AARRRGH!
THE PRINCESS IS USING A DEMON AS A BLACKJACK TO DESTROY THE TREASURE CHEST?!
Wicked Diamond
+
Cloth
=
Blackjack

SHE'S PROBABLY DIY'ING SOMETHING. MAYBE SHE NEEDS A PART FROM THE CHEST.
Hinge! Hinge!
ARRGH!
URGH!
UM... WHAT?!
THAT CAN'T BE! IMPOSSIBLE! SHE'S THE HOSTAGE, ISN'T SHE?!
AS A DEMON, SHOULDN'T YOU BE STOPPING HER?!

klang
klang
klang
klang
klang
klang
...
...
HA! YOU'RE QUITE THE COMEDIAN!
Aha ha ha
I WASN'T TRYING TO BE FUNNY!

UH... UM... I ONLY KNOW THE PRINCESS FROM THE TIMES SHE'S OPENED MY BOOK...
IF THIS BEHAVIOR IS TYPICAL, SHE MUST BE CAUSING YOU DEMONS A LOT OF PROBLEMS.
GRWRR

YEP! WE HAVE CASUAL-TIES EVERY DAY!
WHAT...? CASUAL-TIES...?
YOU HAVE CASU-ALTIES EVERY DAY?!

YOUR DEMON COMPATRIOTS HAVE BEEN KILLED?!
Fear of confirmation bias
Oh!
Yoo hoo!
GRWR
YEP, THAT'S RIGHT. WE HAVE GHOST SHROUD DEATHS DAILY. ABOUT FIVE A DAY, ACTUALLY.
THAT SHOULD NOT BE AN EVERYDAY OCCURENCE!

YEAH, BUT...THE PRINCESS DIES AT LEAST ONCE A WEEK HERSELF.
WHAT?!
I SAID, SHE DIES EVERY WEEK.
...
HEH HEH HEH
Ghost Shroud!
slip
SPLASH
BOB BOB
...
...

Demon retrieval team
SIGH
AIIEEE! THE PRINCESS!

SEE?
WHAT DO YOU MEAN, "SEE?"!

Ahhh...
THE PRINCESS TAKES GREAT RISKS TO ATTACK US, YOU KNOW.
IT WOULD BE A SHAME TO CRAMP HER STYLE.

continue
×∞
BAM
BESIDES, THE DEMON CLERIC HAS GOTTEN USED TO IT.
WHY IS LOSS OF LIFE TREATED SO LIGHTLY IN THIS CASTLE?!

IT'S NOT RIGHT! I MEAN, I'M GLAD THE PRINCESS IS BEING REVIVED OF COURSE, BUT...
SOMETHING STRANGE IS GOING ON... SOMETHING IS AMISS...

COULD IT BE THAT... THE PRINCESS'S CAPTIVITY...
...IS CAUSING HER FAR MORE SUFFERING THAN THOUGHT?
KRAKABOOM

KRAKOOM
WHAT?! H-HAS THE HERO FINALLY ARRIVED ...?
THE PRINCESS! SHE'S BEEN REVIVED AND IS ALREADY WREAKING HAVOC IN THE CASTLE AGAIN!
RMBLRMBLRMBLRMBLRMBL
AND SHE'S HOPPING MAD BECAUSE THAT GHOST SHROUD GOT THE BETTER OF HER JUST NOW!

WE'D BET-TER MAKE A RUN FOR IT. THE BOMB THE PRINCESS HAS EQUIPPED IS POW-ERFUL!
SHE'S EQUIPPED WITH... A BOMB ?!

UM... A BOMB ... WHAT IS SHE PLANNING TO DO WITH A BOMB?!
ARRRGH!
BEATS ME.

YOU KNOW, THE PRINCESS IS ALWAYS CRAFTING SOMETHING... WHAT DO YOU THINK SHE'S MAKING TODAY?
ROLLROLL
ROLLROLL
HOW SHOULD I KNOW?!

THAT WAS HORRI-FYING ...
See ya!

I THOUGHT THE REASON SHE HARDLY EVER USED ME WAS BECAUSE SHE HAD NO INTENTION OF DESTROYING THE DEMONS ...
I NEVER DREAMED THE REASON COULD BE THAT SHE CAN HANDLE THEM ALL ON HER OWN!
drag
drag

IN THAT CASE... MY PRESENCE IS STILL SUPERFLUOUS HERE.
FAREWELL, PRINCESS! I AM DEPARTING ON A JOURNEY TO—

HEY, GRIMOIRE!
BAM
PERFECT TIMING!
?!

I CRAFTED SOMETHING JUST FOR YOU TODAY.
P-PRINCESS?!
FOR ME?!
COULD SHE HAVE HAD A PREMONITION THAT I WAS PLANNING TO ABANDON HER IN THE CASTLE?!

I KNEW IT! THE PRINCESS HAS BEEN CREATING A FIENDISH DEVICE TO EXECUTE ME!
AHHHHH!

TA-DAH! GRIMOIRE, MEET CUSHIONED GRIMOIRE CARRYING CASE!
TA—DAH
...
...

HUH...?
AND THAT'S NOT ALL!

IF WE CLOSE THE CASE LIKE THIS...
GYAK
SQWEEZ

COMPLETED!
THE PORTABLE, VERSATILE GRIMOIRE PILLOW!

AREN'T YOU GLAD YOU CAN BE CARRIED IN STYLE NOW?
UH... UM...
ER... DOES THIS MEAN...
...THE PRINCESS STILL INTENDS TO... MAKE USE OF ME?
...

I DON'T GET IT...
ZZZ...
FWAPP
I DON'T UNDERSTAND THE PRINCESS AT ALL...
I FIND IT...
...SERIOUSLY PROBLEMATIC THAT IT'S A HUNDRED TIMES EASIER TO CONVERSE WITH A DEMON THAN WITH YOU.
Huh?
SOMEDAY MAGAZINE

You've created a cute grimoire.

The Princess Syalis Special Plush Book Cover

Softness: ☆☆☆☆☆☆☆☆
Dreaminess & Stylishness: ☆☆☆☆☆☆☆☆

A versatile book cover inspired by a vague idea that it would be fun to turn Alazif into a pillow because it's handy to have the grimoire nearby.

This is just another of the princess's vast collection of novelty bedding items created from the usual raw materials. But for Alazif, it came as quite a surprise.

Alazif is often seen stroking the soft part of the cushion, so it appears he likes his new cover.

Former problem:
"Demons must die."

Current problem:
"My dignity as a grimoire has plummeted thanks to this book cover."

PRINCESS! I HATE TO SAY THIS, BUT...
...I THINK THERE'S A THING OR TWO YOU COULD STAND TO LEARN FROM THE DEMONS ABOUT COMMUNICATION!
Hmph!
Hmm...
FOR EXAMPLE, THE DEMON I TALKED TO TODAY...
HAR HAR HAR HAR
Ha ha ha
HEH HEH HEH HEH HEH
NEVER MIND...
?

Would you like to change your class?
11 changes remaining
▶Yes
No ▼
Doctor
"I'm going to perform all kinds of operations!"

119th Night: From the Case Files of Sleeping Syalis

Ninety-nine percent of the time...

...the Demon King's problems are caused by the princess's shenanigans.

WHAT? THE PRINCESS IS OPENING A DETECTIVE AGENCY?!

THAT'S RIGHT.

HERE'S THE FLYER.
BAM
SYALIS DETECTIVE AGENCY
I'll solve any mystery!
CLIENT TESTIMONIALS
DROP BY THE PRINCESS'S ROOM FOR HELP AND ADVICE!
SHE'S SERIOUS!
WHAT IS THE MEANING OF THIS?!
REGARDLESS, IT CAN ONLY END IN DISASTER... I MUST PUT A STOP TO THIS!
WHAM
HEY, PRINCESS! WHAT ARE YOU MESSING AROUND WITH THIS TIME?!
THE DETECTIVE IS IN

TA DAH
URK?!
HAVEN'T YOU EVER HEARD OF...
...AN ARMCHAIR DETECTIVE?

WHAT?! Y-YES...
AN ARMCHAIR DETECTIVE...
...IS A SUPERCOOL INVESTIGATOR WHO DOESN'T GO TO THE SCENE OF THE CRIME...
...BUT SOLVES CASES WHILE ROCKING IN AN ARMCHAIR—OR EVEN LYING IN BED!

IN OTHER WORDS... AN ARMCHAIR DETECTIVE IS...
...THE PERFECT JOB TO ENHANCE YOUR REPUTATION WHILE YOU SLEEP!
I DON'T THINK THAT'S HOW IT WORKS!
You're supposed to be **awake** while solving the cases!

119th Night: From the Case Files of Sleeping Syalis

ANYWAY, PRINCESS, THE DEMON CASTLE ISN'T IN NEED OF ANY DETECTIVES.
THERE AREN'T ANY DEMONS WITH MYSTERIES TO SOLVE UNDER MY CASTLE ROOF.
FWP
YOU CAN PUT OUT A CALL FOR CLIENTS, BUT YOU'LL NEVER GET–

WHOA... YOU HAVE A LOT OF CUSTOMERS!
CHTTR
CHTTR

WHAT ..?
I HAD NO IDEA THE DEMON CASTLE STAFF HAD SO MANY PROB-LEMS...
H-HEY, PRINCESS! THERE'S A HUGE LINE OUTSIDE ...

SHE'S ASLEEP!
AS USUAL

PRIN-CESS! H-HEY!
WHAT SHOULD I DO? JUST IGNORE THIS AND LEAVE?
wakka
wakka
BUT EVERY-ONE HERE HAS A PROBLEM THAT NEEDS SOLVING ...

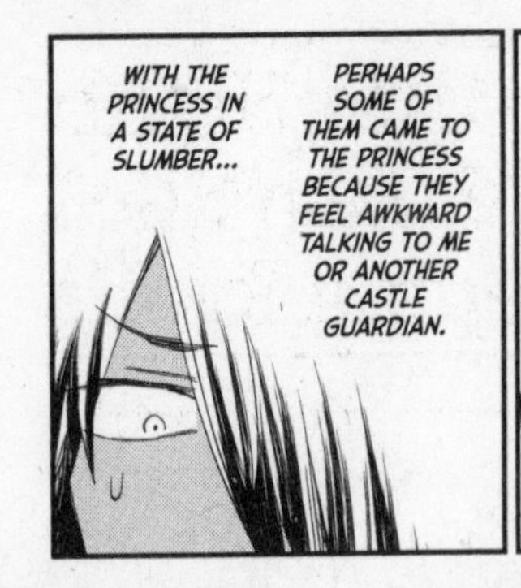
PERHAPS SOME OF THEM CAME TO THE PRINCESS BECAUSE THEY FEEL AWKWARD TALKING TO ME OR ANOTHER CASTLE GUARDIAN.
WITH THE PRINCESS IN A STATE OF SLUMBER...

...IT SEEMS I HAVE NO CHOICE...
HEY, PRIN-CESS! WE'RE COMING IN, OKAY?

K-CHAK

AS THEIR KING ...
...I MUST EXTEND A HELPING HAND TO THEM!
THE TECTIVE IS IN

First clients
BAM
HOWEVER... I HAVE NO IDEA WHAT SORTS OF REQUESTS THEY'LL MAKE. WHAT IF THEIR PROBLEMS ARE TOO BIG FOR ME TO HANDLE?

MY PROB-LEM IS...
YOUR PROB-LEM IS...?!

I FORGOT WHERE... THE NEW WEAPONS ARE STORED...
Sear-ches
Lord of the castle
THIS MYSTERY COULDN'T HAVE BEEN SIMPLER.

GOOD! I CAN HANDLE THIS...
BUT HOW DO I CON-VEY THE SOLUTION TO HIM? I CAN'T SPEAK IN MY OWN VOICE...

...
...

THEY'RE INSIDE THE ARMORY... IN THE BASEMENT. (FALSETTO VOICE)
REALLY?! GREAT! THANKS!
GOOD. SPEAKING IN FALSETTO APPEARS TO HAVE DONE THE TRICK. NEXT...
Second client
BAM
I WANT TO KNOW WHAT THE SPECIAL OFF-THE-MENU DISH IS IN THE DEMON CASTLE CAFETERIA.
Investigations
WHY ARE THEIR PROBLEMS ALL SO TRIVIAL?!

HMM... WELL, AT LEAST I CAN HANDLE THEM SO FAR.
ZLOOP
SWAY
AAHHHHHHHHHH
A bump in the road

SO, YEAH, I HEARD IT'S REALLY YUMMY, AND...
WHAT THE–? HEY!
RRRL
RRRL
SHOOT! SHE'S IN NO CONDITION TO TAKE ANY MORE CLIENTS!
PRINCESS! HEY!

OH WELL. I GUESS I'LL JUST HAVE TO PUSH HER BACK UPRIGHT...
SHUV

HER WRIST IS SO DELICATE AND FRAGILE!

ZLOOP
PUSH
PUSH
UM... I DON'T THINK IT'S SAFE FOR ME TO GRASP IT! BUT I HAVE TO USE SOMETHING FOR LEVERAGE ...

SWISH
PRINCESS... YOUR HAIR...
IT'S SO SILKY SMOOTH ...
PRIN-CESS ...?
ARCH!

OH!
TO GET THE OFF-MENU DISH, ALL YOU HAVE TO DO IS ASK FOR THE SAME DISH THE PRINCESS ALWAYS ORDERS.
THANKS!

PHEW... ANOTHER CLIENT GONE.
I MANAGED TO PULL IT OFF, BUT... PRINCESS! HEY! I NEED YOU TO SIT UP STRAIGHT ON YOUR OWN!
...

I'M ... ...A GE-NIUS ...
DAMN THIS HOS-TAGE!

Third client
EX-CUSE ME!
...
Y-YES?

PRIN-CESS... YOU KIND OF SOUND LIKE A MAN.
?
NOOOO!

I G-GUESS THAT DIDN'T SOUND ANY BETTER...
ANYWHO... MY PROBLEM IS THAT I'VE LOST MY BRAND-NEW SUNGLASSES.
WHSPR
PRINCESS! TELL HIM, "THEY'RE ON YOUR HEAD!"
HRMGH...?
OH, SHE CAN'T HEAR ME. I'LL HAVE TO GET CLOSER.

TELL HIM, "YOUR SUN-GLASSES ARE ON YOUR HEAD."
WHSPR
...?
ARGH... SHE STILL CAN'T HEAR ME!!
"THE SUN-GLASSES ARE ON YOUR HEAD"!
WHAT?! I'M TOO CLOSE, BUT I HAVE NO CHOICE.
...
I HAVE TO BE CAREFUL NOT TO BREATHE IN HER EAR...

HRMPH.
TWTCH

SORRYYYY!

AHHH!! WHAT AM I APOLO-GIZING TO HER FOR?!
SUN-GLASSES... ON YOUR... HEAD...
OH, YOU'RE RIGHT!
FINAL-LY!!
And so...

Detective Syalis's fame spread through-out the Demon Castle.
THE CULPRIT WAS... YOU.
WOW! SHE'S SLEEPING, YET HER DEDUC-TIONS ARE SO PRECISE!
SHE'S... SLEEPING SYALIS!
SEEMS LIKE I'VE HEARD THAT EPITHET SOME-WHERE BEFORE* ...

PHEW... I'VE DEALT WITH EVERY ONE OF THEIR CASES.
I CAN'T BELIEVE YOU, PRINCESS ...
ARGH
YAWWWN

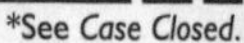
*See *Case Closed*.

I SLEPT THROUGH IT ALL...
...BUT MY WORK HERE IS DONE!
YOU HAVE NO IDEA WHAT YOU PUT ME THROUGH, DAMMIT...
HMPH...
JUST KIDDING... THANK YOU!
YOU SOLVED ALL THE MYSTERIES, DIDN'T YOU?

BECAUSE YOU'RE ALWAYS KEEPING A WATCHFUL EYE ON EVERYONE.
THAT'S WHY YOU'RE THE DEMON KING!
?!

HUH? IT'S GRATIFYING TO HEAR HER SAY IT, ACTUALLY...
IT WAS N-NOTHING, THE CASES WERE ALL PRETTY EASY.
W-WAIT, WHAT?! WHY ARE YOU PRAISING ME ALL OF A SUDDEN...?
WELL...
A GOOD DETECTIVE HAS INTEGRITY AND GIVES CREDIT TO HER SIDEKICK WHERE CREDIT IS DUE.
HUH?
AND NOW... IT'S TIME FOR ME TO REST.

GOOD NIGHT...
...DR. WATSON!
WHO ARE YOU CALLING WATSON?!

ZZZZ...
YOU'RE GOING TO SLEEP AGAIN, PRINCESS?!

The next day...

People lined up before Sleeping Syalis once more...
SOMEBODY STOLE MY SNACK! I WANT YOU TO FIND THE CULPRIT!

...
I HAVEN'T THE FOGGIEST.

But her brilliant deductive powers were never to be seen again.
WHAAAAAT~?!
SHOULD I HELP HER...?

Syalis Detective Agency

Case Closed: ☆☆☆☆☆
Irresponsibleness: ☆☆☆☆☆☆☆☆☆☆☆

A detective agency established by Princess Syalis because she wanted to become an armchair detective. (Self-accredited agency.)

The work was actually carried out by Detective Demon King Twilight instead of Detective Hostage Syalis because the president of the agency didn't do her job.

There was a world of difference between the Demon King's solutions to the cases vs. Princess Syalis's, so clients have mixed reviews of the agency.

It doesn't make sense for the demons to ask the princess for advice in the first place since she is their hostage. They really need to stop turning to her for help.

Maybe I should change my class?

Problem at the outset:
"I had no idea there were so many troubled demons in the Demon Castle..."

Subsequent problem:
"Why are all the problems of the Demon Castle staff so trivial and low stakes?"

I MAY HAVE TO ADD A SECOND CAREER AS A DETECTIVE TO MY DEMON KING JOB...
...!

UM... IF YOU WANT, I'LL GLADLY ASSIST YOU AS A POLICE DOG (?).
AWW... WHO'S A GOOD DOG?!
What loyalty ...

Would you like to change your class?
10 changes remaining
▶ Yes
No ▼
Ghost Buster
"Who you gonna call to get those Ghost Shrouds?!"

120th Night: The First Cut Is the Deepest

Have you ever had this experience ...?

You look into the mirror late at night...

...and you can't fall asleep because your bangs are bugging you.

SNIP

...

At the cafeteria ...
WOW, IT SURE IS CROWDED TODAY!
DEMON CASTLE CAFETERIA
BLAH
BLAH

NOTHING OF NOTE HAS HAPPENED... NOW THAT'S WHAT I CALL A GOOD DAY!
YOU SAID IT!
BLAH
BLAH

I HOPE THE REST OF THE DAY GOES BY JUST AS PEACE-FULLY...

Steamed Monster Bird Egg Custard
Demon Castle Ramen

120th Night: The First Cut Is the Deepest

Castle Ramen
WHOA! WHAT HAP-PENED TO HER BANGS ?!
The demons thoughts are completely in synch.

TUP..
TUP..

THREE STEAMED EGG CUSTARDS, PLEASE.
WAIT... THE PRINCESS IS ACTING AS IF NOTHING HAP-PENED.
SHE MUST HAVE CUT HER BANGS HERSELF. MAYBE SHE DOESN'T THINK SHE SCREWED THEM UP.

YEAH... SHE'S HER USUAL SELF—
WHAT?!
HE'S MAKING YOU GUYS CUT BRUSH ON THE FRINGES OF THE CASTLE GROUNDS?
TWTCH
YOU SHOULD GET HAZARD PAY FOR THAT!

OH, THEY'RE TALKING ABOUT WAGES...

...
...

WHOA! THEY'RE TOTALLY DIFFERENT LENGTHS!
TRMBL

OH.
YOU'RE TERRIBLE AT SPLITTING PAIRS OF CHOPSTICKS IN HALF.

THEY'RE JUST TALKING ABOUT CHOP-STICKS ...
SHE'S CLEARLY UPSET ABOUT HER BANGS!

fwweeghh...
fweergh...
SHE'S GUTTED, BUT SHE'S PRETENDING SHE DOESN'T CARE.
She's a terrible whistler.

IT S-SEEMS THE PRINCESS HASN'T REALIZED THAT WE'VE NOTICED THE PROBLEM WITH HER BANGS...
They haven't noticed.
ALL CONVERSATIONS ABOUT BANGS OR FRINGES OR WHAT-EVER YOU CALL THEM MUST BE BANNED. THEY SAY A WOMAN'S HAIR IS HER CROWN AND GLORY... SO WE NEED TO AVOID TALKING ABOUT HERS AT ANY COST.

I'D LIKE A SPOON, PLEA...
WHIP
PFFFT!!!

OOPS...

...
...

IS SOME-THING WRONG ...?
trmbl trmbl
I'M SORRY!

STAAARE
STAAARE
NO, NO... NOTHING AT ALL. I JUST CHOKED FOR A MOMENT THERE...
STOP! YOU CAN'T BLAME ME!
IT WAS HER FAULT FOR TURNING AROUND ALL OF A SUD-DEN!!

H-HEY, PRINCESS... YOU NEED A SPOON, DON'T YOU? HERE YOU GO...
TRMBL TRMBL
OH. THANKS.

A sigh of relief spreads through the assembled demons.
KLANK...
KLINK...
KLANK...
HUH...? WHAT'S THAT SOUND...?

KLANK
KLINK
fidget
fidget
YUMMY...
*She hasn't eaten a bite yet.
I KIND OF FEEL SORRY FOR HER...

ARGH... LET'S JUST RIP OFF THE BAND-AID AND TELL HER WE ALL NOTICED!
KLTTTR
HOLD ON!

NO, I'M GOING TO TELL HER! EVEN THOUGH SHE'S TRYING TO PUSH IT DOWN WITH HER HAIR BAND, WE CAN STILL TELL HER FRINGE ISN'T STRAIGHT!
SKWEEZ
STOP IT! IT'S POINTING OUT THOSE LITTLE FLAWS THAT DOES THE MOST DAMAGE!

BUT LOOK AT HER! SHE'S SO UPSET ABOUT HER BANGS THAT SHE'S EATING THIN AIR!
YES, I SEE THAT, BUT...
YOU, IDIOT!
Empty

WHAT IF SHE DOES THE SAME THING TO OUR BANGS?!
IT COULD HAPPEN.
Out
Out
Safe

WHY DOESN'T SOMEONE GO OVER AND START A CONVERSATION WITH HER ABOUT SOME OTHER TOPIC TO CHEER HER UP?
GOOD POINT!
SNEAK SNEAK
OH, I'LL GO!
DEFINITELY NOT YOU!!
IF YOU STAND NEXT TO HER, IT'LL LOOK LIKE A BEFORE AND AFTER HAIRCUT SHOT!
Before
After
Ohhhh...

HEY... THEY DON'T THINK MY FRINGE LOOKS FUNNY, DO THEY?
SHAKE SHAKE
GRWR!
A KIND WHITE LIE...
NO, TEDDY DEMON PROBABLY HASN'T GOT AN INKLING WHAT'S GOING ON.
THANK YOU FOR THE MEAL.

And so...
Good night, all...
PHEEEW
WE MANAGED TO GET THROUGH IT SOMEHOW!
The demons' gallantry soothed the princess.
TUP TUP

WHAT A RELIEF... IT SEEMS THEY DIDN'T NOTICE ANYTHING AMISS.
I SUPPOSE I WAS TOO SELF-CONSCIOUS. THAT'S A LOAD OFF MY MIND ANYWAY!

I GUESS DEMONS...
...DON'T GIVE A SECOND THOUGHT TO HUMAN HAIRSTYLES.
OH, PRINCESS!
YOU'VE CUT YOUR FRINGE!

YOU CUT THE CENTER 1.2 INCHES SHORTER AND THE EDGES HALF AN INCH.
Demon Cleric believes it is good manners to comment on changes in a woman's hairstyle.

HYYUR... HYYUR...
HYYURR ?

HYYURRRGH!
WHAMM
SPINNN
ARRRRGH!!

TMP TMP TMP
W-WHAT THE?! PRIN-CESS?! PRIN-CEEEESS?!

SLAM
I KNEW IT!
I SHOULDN'T HAVE GIVEN MYSELF A SLAPDASH HAIRCUT IN THE DARK!

IF I SLEEP A LOT...
...MAY-BE MY FRINGE WILL GROW MORE QUICK-LY...
TUG
TUG

Z-ZZZ...

The next day...

TA-DAH
Gifts
Hair Care
BEAUTEOUS Hair Potion
DEMON SEAWEE
FOR YOUR HAIR
HAIR GROW

MNCH MNCH
WHO...
MNCH
...LEFT THESE HERE?
HMM—...
The princess resolved to ask a profes-sional to cut her hair next time.

The princess's ♡ beauty lesson ♡

It looks the same as before? If the princess says, "My hair has grown back out," then it has!

① First, look into a mirror before you go to sleep.
"Oh, my hair is getting long!"
Now you have insomnia, don't you?

I do!

② Take a pair of scissors. An ordinary pair you use for arts and crafts is fine. It's a pain to find special ones for cutting hair.

Um...

③ Everything is ready now! Grab your bangs and chop them off sideways! What a lovely sound! Now look into the mirror...

Before
After

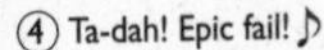
④ Ta-dah! Epic fail! ♪

No surprise there. ♪

DID YOU CUT THE PRINCESS'S FRINGE?
OH MY!
NOT THIS TI-
YOU'RE AN EX-PERT...
...HAIR-DRESSER, AREN'T YOU?
It looks great!
Sincere
Pitying look

Would you like to change your class?
9 changes remaining
▶ Yes
No
Ballerina
"Th-this isn't for me..."

121st Night: Off Duty at the Demon Castle

The princess has been thinking...
I'VE CONQUERED (REPURPOSED FOR BEDDING)...
...NUMEROUS FURRY CREATURES...

...BUT NOW THAT WE'RE DEEP INTO AUTUMN...
...THE TIME HAS COME FOR ME TO CONQUER THE ONE FURRY THING THAT I HAVE YET TO TAME.
WHAT? YOU WANT TO WATCH RED* GO ABOUT HIS DAILY DUTIES?!
UH-HUH.
I WANT TO GET CLOSER TO FURRY DOG...
N-NO! HE WON'T BE ABLE TO GET ANY WORK DONE WITH YOU AROUND, PRINCESS!
Suddenly the Demon King realizes...

*Great Red Siberian

WAIT... HE WON'T BE ABLE TO GET ANY WORK DONE... THAT MIGHT BE JUST THE THING!
GREAT RED SIBERIAN NEVER TAKES A BREAK, NO MATTER HOW OFTEN I TELL HIM TO.
THIS COULD BE A FORTUITOUS OPPORTUNITY TO PREVENT MY BELOVED DOG FROM DYING OF OVERWORK!
And so...

I HAVE TO TAKE THE WHOLE DAY OFF...?
THAT'S RIGHT. HAVE A NICE REST.
AND ALSO... UM...

... SPEND THE DAY WITH... ...THE PRINCESS ...

121st Night: Off Duty at the Demon Castle

WHAT?! WITH THE PRINCESS ...?
...
I CAN'T BELIEVE MY EARS!
...

WHY ?!
C-CALM DOWN! I KNOW WHAT YOU'RE THINKING ...
BUT YOU'LL EVEN WORK THROUGH HOLIDAYS IF I DON'T TAKE DRASTIC MEASURES LIKE THIS.
I'VE RUN OUT OF IDEAS ...
B-BUT, I...
THIS IS AN ORDER! EVERY DAY IS THE WEEKEND FOR THE PRINCESS. HAVE HER TEACH YOU HOW TO WHILE THE DAY AWAY!
Huh?
Weekend

ALL RIGHTIE THEN... I'M OFF TO WORK!
M-MY LIEGE ...!
SLAM
W-WHY IS HE ...
... MAKING ME...
... SPEND THE DAY WITH...
...THE PRINCESS?!

LET'S BE CRAZY LAZY ALL DAY!
THIS IS STRESS-FUL!!

AHHH! THIS IS RIDICULOUS!
I KNOW MY KING ORDERED ME TO DO THIS, BUT IT'S HUMILIATING TO BE SCHOOLED BY THE PRINCESS!
I'M JUST SUPPOSED TO ENJOY MY BREAK, RIGHT? I CAN DO THAT WITHOUT HELP!

WHAT DO YOU NORMALLY DO WHEN YOU'RE OFF WORK?
ORGANIZE DOCUMENTS.
SLAM
ACTUALLY, THAT'S WORK.

WHAT ELSE...?
BATTLE TRAINING!
SLAM
THAT'S WORK TOO.
...
...

IT SEEMS TO ME...
...YOU DON'T EVER REALLY TAKE A BREAK.
RIGHT...
Red is an obedient woof woof.

I CAN'T OBEY MY LIEGE'S ORDERS...
FIRST YOU HAVE TO DO SOME-THING ABOUT YOUR ENSEM-BLE...
MY WHAT...?!

IF YOU WALK AROUND IN THAT, IT WON'T BE CLEAR THAT YOU'RE NOT WORKING. YOUR SUBOR-DINATES WILL ASK YOU TO DO THINGS FOR THEM.
R-RIGHT...
SURPRIS-INGLY, THAT'S A GOOD POINT.
MAYBE THE PRINCESS'S EXTENSIVE EXPERIENCE RELAXING DOES QUALIFY HER TO GIVE AD-VICE ON THE SUBJECT...

YOU'RE TAKING THE DAY OFF... SO LET'S GO FOR A LOOK WITH A POWERFUL VACATION VIBE.
POWERFUL VACATION VIBE?

CHTTR

...
TA
DA
...
...
CHTTR
CHTTR
CHTTR
CHTTR
CHTTR
CHTTR
CHTTR

DO I LOOK ALL RIGHT ...?
HEY, PRINCESS! ARE YOU SURE ABOUT THIS VACATION OUTFIT?!
CHTTR CHTTR
SURE ...
CHTTR
BECAUSE IT SEEMS LIKE EVERYONE IS CONFUSED ABOUT OUR APPEARANCE...
CHTTR
WHAT HAPPENED ...?
DID HE DRINK A BAD POTION ...?

...
YOU'RE JUST HEARING THINGS BECAUSE YOU HAVE A GUILTY CONSCIENCE ABOUT BEING THE ONLY ONE NOT WORKING.
I'M HEARING THINGS?!
LET'S PLAY SOME MUSIC TO DROWN OUT THE VOICES IN YOUR HEAD.
BAM
CHAKKA BOOM
CHAKKA BOOM
CHAKKA BOOM
CHAKKA BOOM

THIS CAN'T BE RIGHT! I'M SURE OF IT!
HEY, PRINCESS! I'VE NEVER SEEN A DEMON BEHAVE LIKE THIS IN THE CASTLE BEFORE! YOU'RE MAKING THIS UP, AREN'T YOU...?
TUP TUP
NO. NORMALLY THEY GO TO TOWN IN THEIR VACATION CLOTHES.
SO NATURALLY YOU WOULDN'T SEE THEM IN THE CASTLE.
...
...
Party animal...
Party animal...

I SEE...
Red is an understanding dog.
?
B-BUT THESE CLOTHES ARE SO...
IT SEEMS YOU STILL FEEL GUILTY ABOUT TAKING TIME OFF.
SO LET'S SAY YOU'RE TAKING A BREAK DUE TO AN INJURY, OKAY?
WHAT...?

TA DAH
Drew them on
I FEEL EVEN WORSE NOW!

HEY, ARE YOU POSITIVE ABOUT THIS?! I'M NOT MAKING A BIG MISTAKE, AM I?!
HE'S DEFINITELY YAKUZA...
I'M SCARED... I'M SCARED...
Demon Army troops
HMM...
YOUR INJURY MIGHT LOOK A LITTLE TOO SERIOUS...

TA DAH
SO LET'S SHOW THEM WE'RE HAVING FUN!
THAT'S A YAKUZA WHO WENT TO AN AMUSEMENT PARK...
YEP. DEFINITELY A YAKUZA WHO WENT TO AN AMUSEMENT PARK...
HEY, PRINCESS... ARE YOU SURE THESE ARE REAL VACATION CLOTHES?!
FAST PASS
POP CORN

SIGH... WELL, I MANAGED TO GET THROUGH THE WHOLE DAY WITHOUT WORKING. I'VE TAKEN A REAL BREAK!
LET'S TAKE A NAP NEXT. THEN YOU'LL HAVE PERFECTED THE ART OF LOAFING!
And here is...
...your bed.
AND I'LL GET TO ENJOY YOUR FURRINESS...
BUT HOW IS IT OKAY FOR ME, THE PET DOG, TO BE THE ONLY ONE TAKING THE DAY OFF?!

!
What a worrywart.
AM I NOT NEEDED ANYMORE?! IS THAT IT?!

SIGH... I GUESS IT'S POINTLESS TO DISCUSS SUCH CONCERNS WITH THE PRINCESS.
EVEN THOUGH THAT'S THE REAL REASON I DON'T TAKE TIME OFF FROM WORK...
NEVER MIND WHAT I SAID...
YOU'RE WRONG.

HUH?
COME ON!
WORRY JUST GIVES YOU INSOMNIA.
LIE DOWN!
...

THE DEMON KING WANTS YOU TO TAKE TIME OFF SO YOU'LL BE HEALTHY AND SPEND MORE TIME WITH HIM.
SO TAKE A NAP! NOW!

...!
...

AREN'T YOU GOING TO SLEEP TOO, PRINCESS...?
UM... AFTER YOU...
?
HUH? SHE'S AWFULLY INSISTENT ON ME SLEEPING FOR SOME REASON...

BUT WHAT SHE JUST SAID ABOUT MY MASTER...
...IS A COMFORT...

PRINCESS... I ENJOYED OUR VACATION TODAY...
ZZZ...

I'M GRATEFUL TO Y...
YAY! HE FINALLY FELL ASLEEP!
FLOOOF

I've unburdened myself, yet I feel weighed down...
AHH... THE FURRINESS IS JUST LIKE I IMAGINED!

The next day...
DID YOU GET SOME REST YESTERDAY?
YES, SIR!

THE PRINCESS WAS MORE HELPFUL THAN I EXPEC...
Oh.
Uh-huh...
WAG WAG

OH!
WAG
WAG
D-DID YOU WAG YOUR TAIL AT THE PRINCESS JUST NOW–?
OF COURSE NOT! YOU'RE IMAGINING THINGS! I'VE GOT WORK TO DO!
Go back to your cell, Princess!
Tee Hee
"Maybe someday I'll be able to completely tame (use as a bed pillow) Furry Dog if I keep this up," thinks the princess to herself...
...with a big grin on her face.

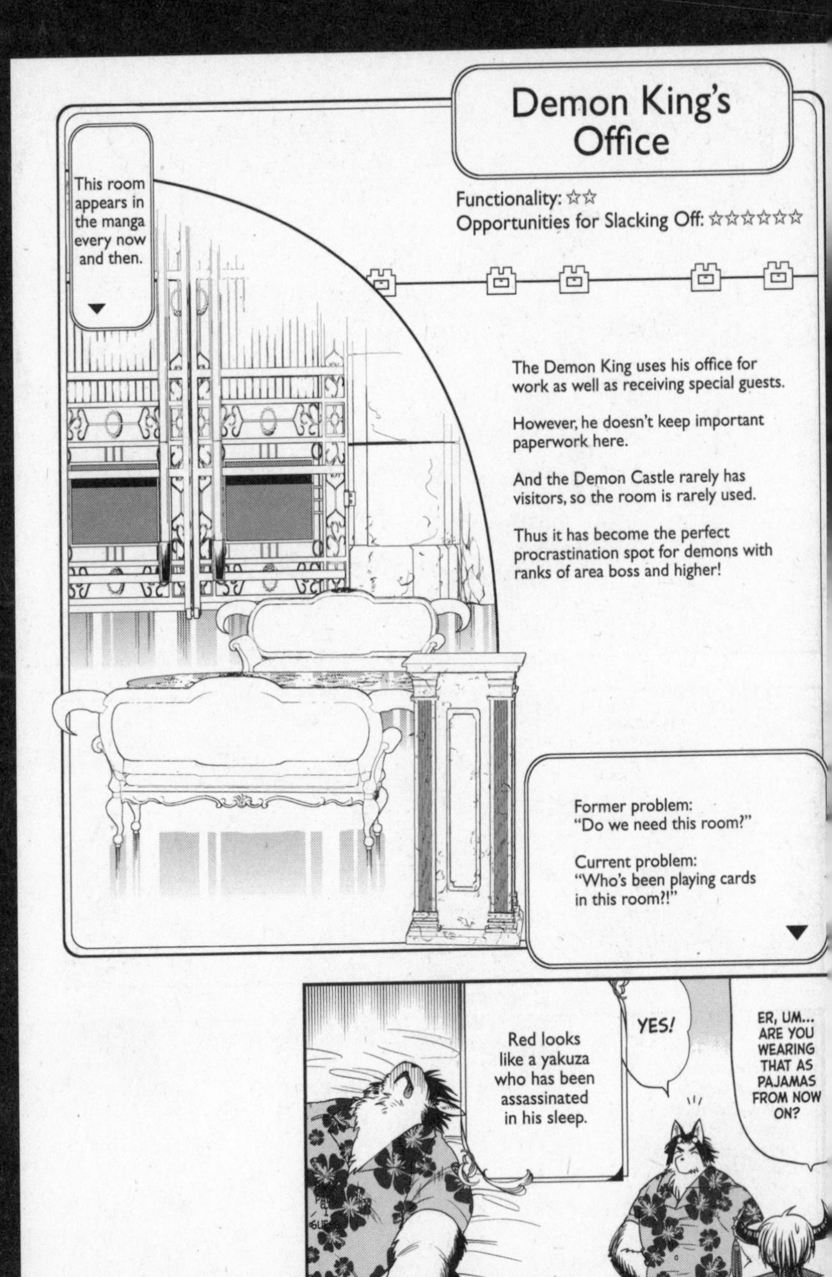
Demon King's Office
Functionality: ☆☆
Opportunities for Slacking Off: ☆☆☆☆☆☆☆
This room appears in the manga every now and then.
The Demon King uses his office for work as well as receiving special guests.
However, he doesn't keep important paperwork here.
And the Demon Castle rarely has visitors, so the room is rarely used.
Thus it has become the perfect procrastination spot for demons with ranks of area boss and higher!
Former problem: "Do we need this room?"
Current problem: "Who's been playing cards in this room?!"
ER, UM... ARE YOU WEARING THAT AS PAJAMAS FROM NOW ON?
YES!
Red looks like a yakuza who has been assassinated in his sleep.

Would you like to change your class?
8 changes remaining
▶Yes
No
Rapper
"Yo, demons are my homies!"

122nd Night: Major PTA Meeting

A trivial quarrel is underway...
WHAT?!

NO WAY!
I'M EGGPLANT SEAL'S BEST FRIEND, SO I GET TO SLEEP WITH IT!

NO! IT WANTS TO SLEEP WITH ME...
...BECAUSE EGGPLANT SEAL LIKES ME BETTER THAN YOU!

Unfortunately, there are witnesses.
CHECKING FOR BROKEN THINGS TO REPAIR IN THE DEMON CASTLE IS TOUGH WORK...
HUH?
HEY, LOOK!

MY LIEGE! YOU WON'T BELIEVE WHAT WE'VE CAUGHT ON CAMERA!!!
SLAM
WHAT'S THAT? HAS THE PRINCESS BROKEN OUT AGAIN?

HEH HEH... WELL, NOTHING CAN SHOCK US AFTER ALL WE'VE BEEN THROUGH WITH HER.
LET'S TAKE A LOOK-SEE...

BUT ...
...MY LOVE IS GREATER!!

?!
*For Eggplant Seal
...
YOU'RE WRONG!

And so the watching demons ...
I'M MORE IN LOVE!
*With Eggplant Seal
THE PRINCESS AND POSEIDON HAVE HOOKED UP!!!
...jump to the wrong conclusion.

122nd Night: Major PTA Meeting

W-W-WHAT'S GOING ON?!
LIVE FROM THE DEMON CASTLE, IT'S...
THIS IS A LIVE STREAM?!
A MEETING! QUICK!
CALL AN EMERGENCY MEETING!!

CHTTR
THIS CAN'T BE HAPPENING...
CHTTR

THE DEITY POSEIDON AND THE HUMAN PRINCESS ARE IN LOVE WITH EACH OTHER?!
THIS IS AN UNBELIEVABLE SCANDAL! IT COULD DESTROY THE POWER BALANCE BETWEEN THE DEITIES, DEMONS AND HUMANS!
THIS IS OF FAR GREATER CONCERN THAN ANY BATTLE WITH THE HERO...
THE DEITY SPECIES WHO HAVE KEPT QUIET UNTIL NOW WILL COME STORMING DOWN INTO OUR REALM!

BUT HOW AND WHEN DID THIS HAPPEN?!
WHAT IN THE WORLD ATTRACTED THOSE TWO TO EACH OTHER?!

YOU'RE SO CUTE WHEN YOU SWIM!
ARGH!
YOUR SKIN IS SO SILKY SOFT!
ARRRRGH!!

HEY, DO YOU HAVE ANY EARPLUGS?!
YOU MUST GRIN AND BEAR IT! THIS IS A SERIOUS CRISIS!

THEY'RE REVEALING THE SOURCE OF THEIR LOVE FOR EACH OTHER!
GOD OF THE SEA, MY FOOT!
YEAH...
What they see
Full view
M-MY LIEGE...
I HAVE NO EXPERIENCE WITH SUCH SITUATIONS! WE NEED TO CONSULT SOMEONE MORE MATURE...

I NEVER HAD A CHANCE...
Ha ha ha ha...
I WAS GOING TO ASK DEMON CLERIC, BUT WE'VE LOST HIM...

WAIT!
HUMANS DECLARED THEIR INDEPENDENCE FROM DEITIES LONG AGO.
THEY HAVE NO RIGHT TO FALL IN LOVE NOW.
SO ARE YOU GOING TO BREAK THEM UP OR WHAT?
BUT IT SEEMS...
...THEY'RE DEEPLY IN LOVE.
chttr
chttr

I WANT TO HUG YOU AND SQUEEZE YOU...
I COULD JUST EAT YOU UP...
SQWEE?!
ME TOO... YUMMY WUMMY!
SQWEE!!!
WHAT ARE THEY TALKING ABOUT?!
WHAT'S THAT SQUEALING SOUND IN THE BACKGROUND?
I'VE REPORTED THIS TO HADES!
Poseidon's big brother
OH RIGHT... HIS ELDER BROTHER.
BUT...

...
POSEIDON WOULD NEVER SAY SUCH THINGS.
That's ridiculous.
YOU MUST BE MIS-TAKEN.

...
...

POOR GUY... HE CAN'T HANDLE THE TRUTH.
Ahhh!
THAT'S BECAUSE POSEI-DON IS HIS FLESH AND BLOOD.

WELL, WE'VE GOT A SIMILAR PROBLEM OVER HERE...
IS HE ALIVE ...?

ON THE OTHER HAND, PERHAPS THIS IS AN IMPORTANT PHASE OF EVOLUTION THAT COULD CHANGE ALL OUR SPECIES FOR THE BETTER.
I MUST PAY CLOSE ATTENTION TO EVERYTHING THEY SAY SO AS TO REACH A CONCLUSION.
LET'S SEE WHOSE LOVE IS GREATER ...

ALL WILL BECOME CLEAR TONIGHT IN BED!
*Meaning whoever gets to sleep with Eggplant Seal wins
I DON'T WANT TO LISTEN TO THIS PERSONAL CONVER-SATION ANYMORE!
ARRRRRRGH!

NO!
WE HAVE TO PROVE OUR LOVE RIGHT HERE AND NOW!
STOP!!!
STOP! STOP! THIS IS A MIS-TAKE!
TH-THIS IS A TERRIBLE INVASION OF PRI-VACY...
BLIP

AND WE CAN'T TAKE ANY MORE OF IT!
Devastated

N-NO, WE HAVE TO LIS-TEN!
I don't want to either, but...
WE HAVE TO SEE THIS THROUGH TO THE END!
AHHH...
BIP

VWOOP
IT'S SO SOFT...
IT FEELS SOOO GOOD...

AHHHHH!!
W-WHAT ARE THEY DOING?!
HEY, THE CAMERA IS TOO CLOSE! I CAN'T SEE A THING!
YOU WANT TO SEE THIS?!
NO, I DON'T WANT TO SEE IT, BUT...
My turn! Oh, it is soft...
No way. Oh, it's so smooth.
*Fighting over Eggplant Seal

WHAT CUTE LITTLE FUZZY HAIRS!
WHAT ARE THEY TALKING ABOUT?!

NO, I CAN'T TAKE IT ANYMORE! I CAN'T BEAR TO WATCH!
AHHHH!
VIIP

MY LIEGE... I UNDERSTAND HOW YOU FEEL, BUT YOU MUST CONTINUE.
YOU HAVE TO OBSERVE THEM AND REACH A CONCLUSION.
UM...

THEY'RE RIGHT.
THE FUTURE OF ALL OUR SPECIES DEPENDS ON THE OUTCOME.
I HAVE TO WATCH THIS!
VWIIP
ROLL
...

...
Satisfied look
Satisfied look
D-DID...

DID WE...
...MISS THE MOST IMPORTANT PART?!
NOT THAT I WANTED TO SEE IT!
*Another Eggplant Seal dropped by, which solved the problem.

ZZZ
The meeting continued through the night and a resolution was made not to break up the couple.
The next day...
...they contacted the two in question.
B-BBMP
B-BBMP
B-BMP
However...
WHAT IN THE WORLD ARE YOU TALKING ABOUT?
THAT'S HILARIOUS!
...they just laughed the matter off.

Emergency Demon Castle Meeting

Urgency: ☆☆☆☆
Frequency: ☆☆☆

Silence!

A council meeting at the Demon Castle held not to discuss defense against the humans but rather to review internal matters. All Demon Castle staff are invited to attend, but these meetings were infrequent before the princess arrived and mostly consisted of dry discussions of budget reports. The demon guardians are glad attendance has increased at these meetings since the princess's arrival. Or perhaps not...

Emergency Demon Castle Meeting Agenda (Just a small segment)

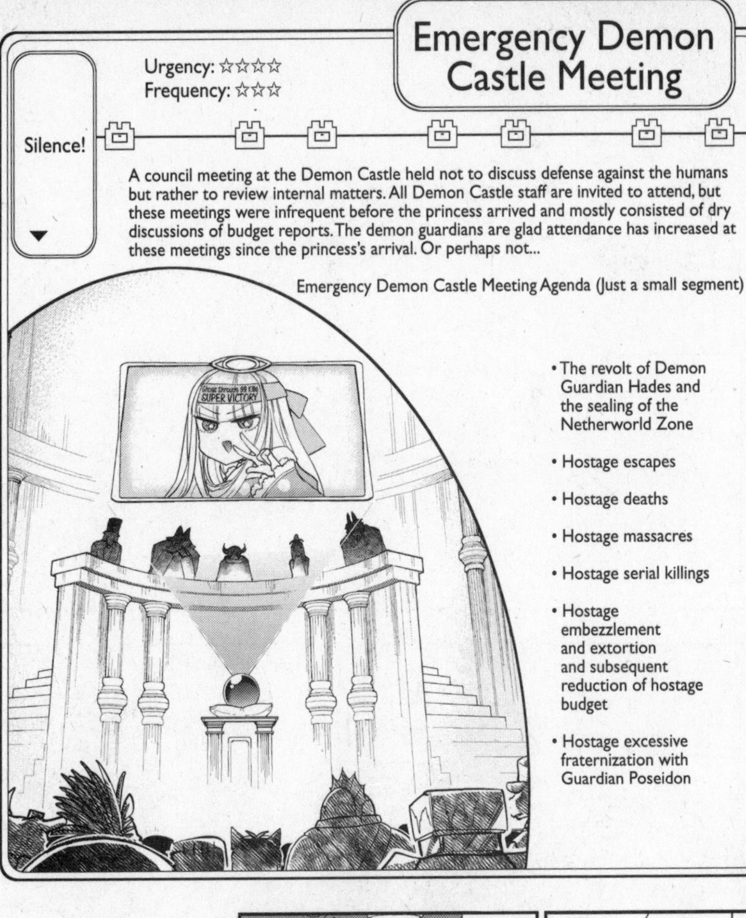
SUPER VICTORY

- The revolt of Demon Guardian Hades and the sealing of the Netherworld Zone
- Hostage escapes
- Hostage deaths
- Hostage massacres
- Hostage serial killings
- Hostage embezzlement and extortion and subsequent reduction of hostage budget
- Hostage excessive fraternization with Guardian Poseidon

Afterwards...
HA HA HA! ME AND THE PRINCESS?! NEVER!
BY THE WAY...
So...
...DO YOU FEEL A CHILL?
Huh?
?
I refuse to believe it...
Somehow they cleared up the misunderstanding.

Would you like to change your class?
7 changes remaining
▶Yes
No
Cabin Attendant
"Chicken or beef?"

123rd Night: Taking the Cat to the Vet

Does the following look familiar...?

AIIEEE!
OH! THERE'S THE CAPTIVE PRINCESS!
THAT'S JUST AN ARTIST'S RENDERING.

HELP... ME...
Images like this...

...are designed to depict the hapless hostage in such a way as to provoke the hero's ire.
A film like this is known as...
...A HERO TROLLING MOVIE! THAT'S WHAT WE'RE GOING TO MAKE!
OOH, A HERO TROLLING MOVIE!

ABOUT TIME!
THAT'S RIGHT! AND WE'LL FILM IT IN THE CANYON OF DEATH.
WE'RE MAKING A FILM ABOUT THE HELPLESS PRINCESS TO RAISE THE HERO'S AWARENESS...
BUT HOW ARE WE GOING TO GET THE PRINCESS OUT THERE...?
WELL...
WHAT...? AN EXCURSION TO VIEW THE AUTUMN FOLIAGE?

THAT'S RIGHT. IT'S THE PERFECT DESTINATION.
VERY CLASSY.
IT WON'T HURT TO GO ON A LITTLE PLEASURE TRIP FOR A CHANGE.
EVEN THOUGH IT'S ALL A LIE!

YOU'RE SO DEMONIC, MY LIEGE!
IT'S THE ONLY WAY. AND THIS IS THE HOSTAGE'S JOB, AFTER ALL...
SO TRUE!

HERE, TAKE A SEAT ON THIS ...
HURRY UP.
WE'LL GET HER THERE AS FAST AS WE CAN SO SHE DOESN'T HAVE A CHANCE TO ESCAPE!
WHAT? WHAT?
WE'RE GOING RIGHT AWAY?

OH, WE'RE ALL GOING TOGETHER...
THAT'S NICE.

AN AUTUMN FOLIAGE EXCURSION, HUH...?
WHAT DID I DO TO DESERVE THIS?

H-HERE WE ARE, PRINCESS!
HMM...
OH... I MUST HAVE FALLEN ASLEEP.

?

123rd Night: Taking the Cat to the Vet

...
...
...
...

HEY ...
WHERE'S THE AUTUMN FOLIAGE ...?

HUH...? AUTUMN FOLIAGE ...
Wander
Wander
WHERE ARE THE FIERY COLORED LEAVES?
NO FOLIAGE AT ALL HERE...
DON'T LOOK AT US LIKE THAT!

N-NO. I MUST KEEP MY RE-SOLVE.
AND FULFILL OUR PURPOSE.
TUP
U-UM... APOLOGIES, PRINCESS!
THE AUTUMN FOLIAGE EXCURSION WAS JUST A LIE TO LURE YOU OUT HERE!

A... LIE?
TH-THAT'S RIGHT!
WE'RE ACTU-ALLY HERE TO FILM A VIDEO FOR THE HERO.
YOU'RE A BIT TOO FAR AWAY THOUGH. COULD YOU STAND ON TOP OF THAT CROSS MARK OVER THERE?

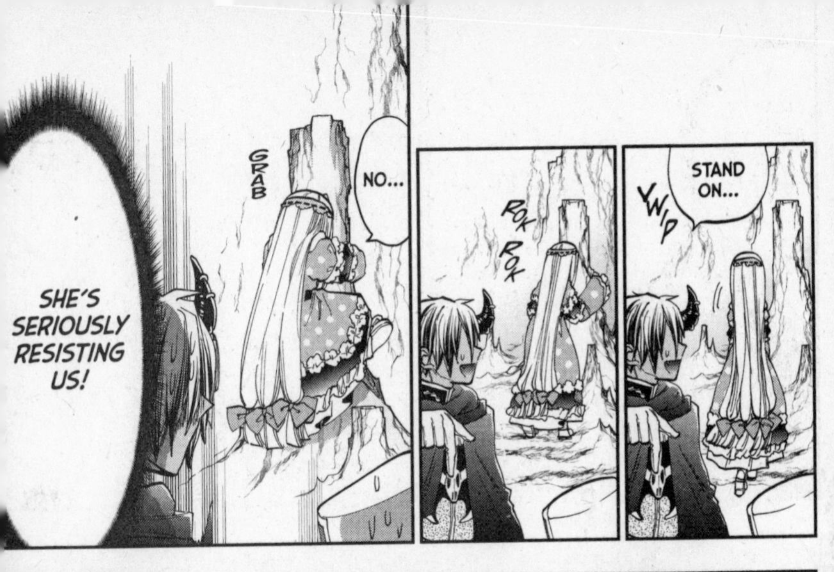
STAND ON...
YWIP
ROK ROK
NO...
GRAB
SHE'S SERIOUSLY RESISTING US!

C-C'MON, PRINCESS! IT'LL BE OVER QUICKLY!
NO.
WE HAVE A SCRIPT FOR YOU! IT'LL BE A PIECE OF CAKE!
NO!
Script
HISSS
DE-MONS ARE LIARS...
I WILL NEVER FOR-GIVE YOU!
THAT HURTS. BUT WE DESERVE IT.

W-WHAT ARE WE GONNA DO? WE'LL NEVER GET IT DONE AT THIS RATE!
WHAT SHOULD WE DO...?
HEY, PRINCESS!

YANK
WE'RE SORRY WE LIED TO YOU, BUT WE'RE NOT GETTING ANYWHERE LIKE THIS!
AT LEAST MOVE TO A SPOT WHERE WE CAN SHOOT SOME VIDEO OF YOU!
STOP IT! LET ME GO!
HELP! KIDNAPPERS!
YOU, YOU... LYING, FURRY WOOF WOOF YOU!
IS THAT MEANT TO BE DEROGATORY?!

I CAN'T BELIEVE IT!
HOW COULD YOU ALL DECEIVE ME LIKE THIS?!
GRAB
OOH, A GINGKO NUT!
WHAT?!
...
WRONG.

IT'S JUST A PEBBLE.
I CAN'T EAT THIS.
WE'RE STARTING TO FEEL SORRY FOR HER!

And so...
PRINCESS! YOU MUSTN'T EAT THE SCRIPT!
RIP
MUNCH
Script
WE CAN'T GET YOU ON CAMERA IF YOU KEEP THROWING YOURSELF ON THE GROUND!
FLOP
GO TO HELL!
Grrrr
The princess continues to resist.
THIS IS THE DEMON WORLD, PRINCESS!
We are in hell!

...
THIS VIDEO SHOOT IS GOING NOWHERE FAST.
Why did you have to lie to her?
I thought we'd be able to work it out once we brought her here...
Autumn foliage...
The princess won't say anything but "autumn foliage" now.

WHAT DO I DO NOW?!
THE PRINCESS HASN'T EVEN STOOD IN FRONT OF THE CAMERA YET!
Keeps flopping down
whuudd
Don't you have bones?!
She's like a dropped rice cake...
I HAD NO IDEA SHE WANTED TO SEE AUTUMN FOLIAGE SO BADLY.
SIIIIIGH...
SHE'S MOSTLY ANGRY BECAUSE WE LIED TO HER...
E-EXCUSE ME...
UM... I'VE ACTUALLY HAD THE CAMERA ROLLING ALL THIS TIME...
...AND I'VE EDITED THE VIDEO A BIT...
WHAT?!

W-WHAT ARE YOU SAYING?
YOU COULDN'T HAVE SHOT ANYTHING WORTHWHILE IN THIS HULLABALOO.

WHAT'S THE POINT OF EDIT-ING IT?
BIP

STOP IT! LET ME GO!
HELP! KIDNAP-PERS!
TA DAH
DE-MONS ARE LIARS...
I'LL NEVER FOR-GIVE YOU!
BAMM

I CAN'T BE-LIEVE IT!
HOW COULD YOU ALL DECEIVE ME LIKE THIS?!
IT'S JUST A PEBBLE.
I CAN'T EAT THIS.
♫WAH WAH WAHHH...♪

...
GO TO HELL!
THE END
...

...
...

HOW DID WE MANAGE TO END UP WITH SUCH EXCELLENT FOOTAGE?!
She looks ...
... pitiful.
NOT A CLUE!
Scri

SLEEP OF EXHAUSTION

And thus...
...the hero trolling movie *The Rise and Fall of the Wrath of Syalis* is completed.

It successfully pulled at the hero's heart-strings.
I
ROMIS
I'LL
SAVE
OU
MATT

The demons are un-aware that...
...coinci-dentally they're about to pass through a mountain covered in autumn foliage on their way back.
Autumn foliage ...

Hero Trolling Movie

What a pitiful hostage!

Effect: ☆☆☆☆☆☆
Filming Difficulty: ☆☆☆☆☆☆☆

This is just one of the plans the demons concocted to motivate the hero on his quest to save the princess.

Such films are used to raise awareness of the hostage's plight and to remind the hero both of the goal of his quest and that he represents humankind, as well as to prevent him from getting sidetracked. Such techniques have been used since the days of yore and are (usually) easy to create.

One reason it was so difficult to make this movie is that the princess is not your average hostage—however, the main reason is that no one pointed out the movie was prerecorded, so they could have just filmed it in the Demon Castle.

Comments from substitute director Vampire:

"Seriously, we could have just shot the movie in the castle! It's not like it's a live stream or anything!"

AIIEEE! PRINCESS! I'M COMING TO SAVE YOU RIGHT AWAY!
GRAB
WAIT, DAWNER!

UM... THE PRINCESS ISN'T ACTUALLY INSIDE THAT CRYSTAL.
YOU KNOW THAT, DON'T YOU?
Right?

Does he think I'm that stupid?
WHY'RE YOU LOOKING AT ME LIKE THAT ...?!

Would you like to change your class?
6 changes remaining
▶Yes
No
2°c
Weather Reporter
"The rain will change to snow at midnight!"

124th Night: Have You Seen Our Princess?

Previously...

The demons lied to the princess. They pretended to take her out on an autumn foliage viewing excursion in order to film a video to motivate the hero on his quest to rescue her.
The princess was furious with the demons for their subterfuge, but they managed to capture the footage they needed nevertheless. Now they are all heading back to the castle...
The princess is still obsessed with viewing autumn foliage.

OKAY, LET'S TAKE A BREAK IN THIS SPOT.
FILMING THAT VIDEO WAS SUCH A HASSLE!
HRM? WHERE ARE WE...?
A MOUNTAIN EN ROUTE TO THE CASTLE.

...
chttr
chttr
!

THAT'S... A RED MAPLE LEAF!

tddl
tddl
tddl
tddl

Oh...
HUH? WHERE'S THE PRINCESS?
...
...

THE PRINCESS ...
...IS GONE!!
124th Night: Have You Seen Our Princess?

DID SHE GET LOST?!
OH! I SEE SOME AUTUMN LEAVES OVER THERE!
SHE MUST HAVE GONE OFF TO SEE THE TURNING LEAVES BY HERSELF!

SPLIT UP AND FIND HER!
Yes, my liege!
WHO KNOWS WHAT TROUBLE SHE'LL GET INTO!
The demons don't imagine for a moment that the princess is attempting to escape.

WHAT?!
A HUMAN GIRL LOST ON THIS MOUNTAIN?!

BUT... HOW?
Local demon
It's the Demon King!
BIG BRO
DUE TO... VARIOUS REASONS!
WE CAN'T TELL HIM WE LOST OUR HOSTAGE!
Aha ha ha
Ha ha ha

SORRY TO HEAR IT. WANT ME TO ASK MY BRO FOR HELP?
YES, PLEASE!
Meanwhile ...

HUH ...?
ARE YOU A HUMAN? OR A DEMON? HMM...
LI'L BRO

RSTL
YOU TOTALLY SMELL LIKE A DEMON!
WHAT?
AND YOU'RE NOT SCARED OF ME AT ALL. WHAT ARE YOU DOING ON THIS MOUNTAIN, LITTLE GIRL?
LI'L BRO
...
← Acclimatized to demons

...
I CAME TO SEE THE AUTUMN FOLIAGE.
...
BUT...

...MY FRIENDS GOT LOST!
IS THAT SO? POOR THING...

I'LL HELP YOU FIND THEM.
BRRRRNG
HUH? HEL-LO...?
LISTEN UP, LITTLE BROTHER...
OH, HELLO, BIG BROTHER! WHAT? A HUMAN GIRL? LOST ON THE MOUNTAIN?

...
STAARE
ATTABOY!
Attagirl! Go, Demon Castle!

NAH, HAVEN'T SEEN HER.
OH, OKAY.

W-WAIT! SHE'S NO ORDINARY GIRL...

HOW CAN I PUT THIS... SHE OBLITERATES EVERYTHING IN HER PATH.
The autumn leaves are so beautiful...♫

SHE HAS A SAVAGE MIND AND COMMITS MASSACRES.
I'll save these gingko nuts to eat with the others.♪

SHE'S A DANGEROUS LEADER OF COUNTLESS BEARS, AS WELL.
LI'L BRO
...
I've gathered so many pretty maple leaves!♪
...

SHE HAS THE POWER TO VAPORIZE ANYTHING WITH THE HELP OF A GRIMOIRE!
Can't... get this... gingko nut shell... open...
...
WAIT! THERE'S MORE!
NOPE. HAVEN'T SEEN ANYONE LIKE THAT.

NO, SERIOUSLY. I REALLY HAVEN'T SEEN HER.
BIG BRO
LI'L BRO
DAMN IT! WHERE COULD SHE BE?!
Near-by...

OH, BY THE WAY, BIG BROTHER... I'M LOOK-ING FOR SOMETHING TOO.
WHAT'S THAT ...?
BIG BRO

WELL ...
HAVE YOU BY ANY CHANCE SEEN A GROUP OF PUPPY-EYED DEMON GUARDIANS?
Princess's description

WHAT ...?
...
BIG BRO

...
Demon King
Guard-ian
Guard-ian
Guard-ian
BIG BRO

NOPE. HAVEN'T SEEN 'EM.
WE HAVEN'T SEEN HIDE NOR HAIR OF THEM EITHER.
SORRY WE CAN'T BE OF ANY HELP.
WAIT! THERE'S MORE!

APPARENTLY ONE OF THEM IS SUPER INNOCENT AND KIND...
...AND TALKS IN A CUTE WAY.
BIG BRO
WHO COULD THAT BE?
Innocent
I HAVE NO IDEA WHAT SORT OF DEMON THAT IS.
ME NEITHER.

THE SECOND ONE IS AN OLD MAN WITH A SOOTHING MANNER.
HE ALSO HAS A CUTE TAIL.
BIG BRO
AN OLD MAN WITH A CUTE TAIL?
Old man
CAN'T FOR THE LIFE OF ME IMAGINE WHAT THAT WOULD LOOK LIKE.
NO IDEA.

AND THE THIRD ONE IS... AN OBEDIENT DOGGY...
...WHO IS VERY FURRY AND SMELLS NICE.
BIG BRO
I WOULD BE ASHAMED TO BE A DOG LIKE THAT DEMON.
Doggy
THAT DOG HAS NO SELF-RESPECT!
RIGHT!

AND THE FOURTH ONE IS... A MIS-CHIEVOUS BOY...
...WHO HAS A THING FOR CUTE CREA-TURES.
BIG BRO
TWTCH
OOH, A WITTLE BIRDIE!
WHAT'S WITH YOU, POSEI-DON?!
Mischievous boy

...
...
BIG BRO
NO. SORRY, I HAVEN'T SEEN ANY-ONE LIKE THAT...
BIG BRO
OH, OKAY...
LI'L BRO
WE HAVEN'T SEEN THEM EITHER.
SORRY WE COULDN'T BE OF ANY HELP.
THANKS ANYWAY.

LI'L BRO
I HOPE YOU FIND WHO YOU'RE LOOKING FOR.

THANKS!
...
...
...
BIG
PRINCEEEEESS?!
HUHHHHHH?!

I CAN'T BELIEVE YOU, PRIN-CESS!
Um, everyone...? We've found the princess.
OH! SORRY! I HAD NO IDEA THIS WAS THE GIRL YOU WERE TALKING ABOUT!
NO NEED TO APOLOGIZE ...
I WAS LISTENING, BUT I DIDN'T GET IT EITHER...

I THOUGHT YOU WERE TALKING ABOUT SOME BARBARIC BOSS BEAR OR SOME-THING.
Massacres Obliterates Dangerous
UMM...
BY THE WAY, I'M NOT MAD AT YOU ANY-MORE.

YOU STOPPED BY THIS MOUNTAIN BECAUSE I WANTED TO SEE THE AUTUMN FOLIAGE SO BADLY, DIDN'T YOU?
HUH?
BUT THEN YOU GOT LOST! HA HA HA!
WHAT?

HERE... I MADE A BED FROM A PILE OF MAPLE LEAVES FOR US. LET'S TAKE A NAP BEFORE WE HEAD BACK TO THE CASTLE.
I picked only clean leaves.
...
...

WELL...
I GUESS WE'RE RECONCILED THEN.

HMPH. THE VIEW IS ACTUALLY PRETTY NICE. I GUESS WE CAN AFFORD TO TAKE A LITTLE BREAK.
IS THAT...
... REALLY HOW...
...THE PRINCESS SEES US?!
NNNN...
And so...

...together they enjoy the beautiful autumn foliage.
But because...
...they were so companionable, a rumor spread throughout the region that the hostage princess might actually be a demon.
Source of rumor
DO I REALLY SMELL LIKE A DEMON?
YOU DO...
sniff sniff

One-Horned Hunter Oni Brothers
Kindness: ☆☆☆☆☆☆☆☆☆
Gossip: ☆☆☆☆☆☆☆☆
You smell like a demon!
LI'L BRO
BIG BRO
Two oni brothers who make their living as hunters in these beautiful mountains covered with maple trees. These two powerful demons rule over the mountain, but they are kind and benevolent.
The oni brothers think the Demon Castle and its environs are very cosmopolitan, so their image of Demon King Twilight is that of a super-hip city boy.
The Demon Castle cafeteria added traditional wild game dishes to their menu after this encounter.
Former problem:
"Big brother, do you have any problems?"
"No."
Current problem:
"Big brother, do you have any problems?"
"No."
I SMELL LIKE... A DEMON...
SMELL LIKE A DEMON...
?
WHAT KIND OF A SMELL IS THAT?!
LIKE STEAMED EGG CUSTARD...?
No...

Would you like to change your class?
5 changes remaining
▶Yes
No
Nomad
"I'm going to sleep in a tent!"

125th Night: I'm Really Sorry

I AM TRIPLE FACE!

I WORK IN THE DEMON CASTLE, BUT I AM SECRETLY ALLIED WITH THE HUMANS.
I PLAY THE ROLES OF THREE DIFFERENT PEOPLE. SOME-ONE HAS YET TO NOTICE.

THAT'S RIGHT...
NO ONE HAS FOUND ME OUT!

125th Night:
I'm Really Sorry

Sleepy Princess in the Demon Castle

NARMIE!

OH! HERE'S THE DOCUMENT YOU REQUESTED.
HEY, THANKS!
HE WORKS HARD.
VIP
PART-TIME ORDINARY DEMON...

PART-TIME ORDINARY HUMAN...
SNEAK
TOP SECRET

AND PART-TIME CHEF AT THE DEMON CASTLE CAFETERIA.
I USE MY THREE DIFFERENT FACES TO MAKE MY LIVING.

AND BECAUSE I AM HALF-HUMAN, HALF-DEMON...

...I REFUSE TO SIT BACK AND WAIT FOR THE HERO TO ARRIVE!

I MYSELF WILL DESTROY THE DEMON ARMY **FROM THE INSIDE,** THUS BRINGING AN END TO THIS ETERNAL WAR BY HANDING VICTORY OVER TO THE HUMANS. I WILL DO SO IN HONOR OF MY HUMAN MOTHER WHO RAISED ME. AND IN ORDER TO ACCOMPLISH MY GOAL...

...I CANNOT ALLOW ANYONE TO DISCOVER MY TRUE IDENTITY!
SNEAK
SNEAK

stare

Staaare

SHE'S FOUND ME OUT!

SHE SAW ME CHANG-ING! IT'S USELESS TO PRETEND NOW!
WHAT SHOULD I DO ...?!
...

WHY IS THAT GUY ALWAYS CHANGING CLOTHES IN WEIRD PLACES ...?
?
Clueless

It's just a short-cut to her cell.
I WISH HE'D MOVE ASIDE.

URK... I WAS CHANGING IN A SPOT WHERE I THOUGHT NO ONE WOULD SEE ME. WHAT IS THE HOSTAGE PRINCESS DOING HERE?
HAS SHE BEEN SPYING ON ME?!
...

STGGR
OH... HE MOVED ASIDE FOR ME.
GRIN
!

SHF...
THAT SMIRK !!
I GET IT NOW ...

PRINCESS ...
YOU ARE THE ONLY ONE IN THE CASTLE WHO HAS SUSSED OUT MY TRUE IDENTITY!
GRIN
Hrrgh!
It was only a polite smile because he made space for her to pass.
SOME-THING IS UNCLEAR TO ME THOUGH ...

THE PRINCESS COMES TO THE CAFETERIA EVERY DAY TO ORDER A STEAMED MONSTER BIRD EGG CUSTARD.
IT DOESN'T MAKE SENSE FOR HER TO EAT THAT EVERY SINGLE DAY!
She just likes steamed egg custard.
IT MUST BE A SUBTLE HINT TO CONVEY THAT SHE KNOWS WHO I AM!
She really, really likes steamed egg custard.

OH!
WAIT A MINUTE! COULD IT BE...? IF I COUNT THE NUMBER OF STEAMED MONSTER BIRD EGG CUSTARDS SHE'S EATEN EVERY WEEK AND CORRELATE IT WITH THE ORDER OF THE LETTERS IN THE ALPHABET...
ELEVEN.
NINE.
TWELVE.
TWELVE.
ELEVEN.
NINE.
FOURTEEN.
SEVEN.
1 2 3 4 5 6 7
A B C D E F G
8 9 10 11 12 13 14
H I J K L M N
15 16 17 18 19 20 21
O P Q R S T U
22 23 24 25 26
V W X Y Z
...
...

KILL KING
Total coincidence
KILL ... KING ...

Next day...
DEMON CASTLE CAFETERIA
TOMORROW MUST BE... THE FATEFUL DAY!
AND THE LAST LETTER OF THIS CODED MESSAGE CAME TODAY! AM I OVERTHINKING THIS? NO...
IS THIS SOME KIND OF CODE INSTRUCTING ME TO KILL THE DEMON KING?!
IS THE PRINCESS PLOTTING TO BRING AN END TO DEMONKIND AS WELL?!

TA DAH

SHE'S WEAR-ING BLACK !!
SHE MEANS BUSI-NESS !!
THAT MUST BE HER MOURNING OUTFIT FOR DEMON KING TWILIGHT BECAUSE SHE PLANS TO KILL HIM TO-DAY!
...

Actually, the Teddy Demons burrowed into her clothes to sleep, and this was the only dress she could extricate from the pile.
THAT'S OKAY. ♡

...
STARE
?!
PRIN-CESS...?! WHAT ARE YOU LOOKING AT?!

HEY, TH-THAT'S DEMON KING TWILIGHT! HER TARGET!
Hungry

BUT THE PRINCESS HAS SUCH A LOOK OF GLEE ON HER FACE...
...
IT'S AS IF KILLING IS AN EVERYDAY EVENT FOR HER!

... THE RAMEN LOOKS GOOD TODAY.
Killing is an everyday event for her, but the princess is focused on something completely different at the moment.

OKAY, I KNOW WHAT I WANT TO ORDER.
SHE'S HERE!
WHAT CAN I GET FOR YOU ...?
Demon Castle Ramen
Steamed Monster Bird Egg Custard
Demon Castle Ramen

!
I'LL HAVE A BOWLFUL OF STEAMED MONSTER BIRD EGG CUSTARD, PLEASE.

I SEE... THE REGULAR SERVING OF STEAMED MONSTER BIRD EGG CUSTARD COMES IN A PLAIN CUP...
BUT THE BOWL OF MONSTER BIRD EGG CUSTARD COMES IN A BOWL WITH... THE DEMON KING'S SEAL ON IT!
COULD HER INTENT ...

...BE ANY CLEARER?!
IF I EAT TOO MUCH CUSTARD, I'LL GET SLEEPY.
Hungry

PRINCESS, MESSAGE RECEIVED!
WE SHARE A COMMON GOAL!
I WILL SEND A MESSAGE TO YOU MYSELF.

NOW... WHAT IS YOUR ANSWER?!
LIFT

HOWKILL?
Green onion garnish

...

...

...

CHOMP
MUNCH

Yum, yum!
Bon appétit...
... ...

That was delicious!
P-Princess... did you see my message?
HEH ...

OH, I SEE ...

"NOW IS NOT THE TIME."
THAT'S THE MESSAGE SHE'S CONVEYING TO ME!
She's just full.

NNNN...
I DIDN'T ASSASSINATE THE DEMON KING TODAY...
...BUT I WILL LIVE ON AS... TRIPLE FACE!
rstl
rstl
I'LL CONTINUE MY COVERT SURVEILLANCE UNTIL THE NEXT OPPORTUNITY ARISES...

fwap
WOW... THIS IS GREAT REFERENCE MATERIAL...
Hey, do you guys do inscriptions on your food with toppings?
No.

Triple
Face

Narmie

Sinfulness: ☆☆☆☆☆☆☆☆☆☆☆

Déjà Vu: ☆☆☆☆☆☆☆☆☆☆☆

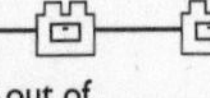

Someone who makes the most out of playing three roles as a part-time ordinary demon, part-time human and part-time Demon Castle Cafeteria chef.

His origin as half-demon, half-human is quite rare. He could have parlayed his heritage to rise to a relatively high position in the Demon Army, but he was raised by a single human mother, so he wholly identifies with his human side.

Then again, he can't get himself to think badly of his coworkers, who have become his friends, so he tries to cure his ambivalence by studying a certain character in his favorite manga.

An avid reader of *Weekly Shonen Someday*.

Current problem:
"I've started out by looking like him, but I think I'm still missing something..."

AH! COULD IT BE THAT... DOES THE PRINCESS...

DOES SHE...

...JUST LIKE TO...
...EAT STEAMED EGG CUSTARD?!

Would you like to change your class?
4 changes remaining
▶Yes
No
Student
"Life is short. Fall asleep, Sya. ♡"

WHAT?!
THE OLD DEMON CASTLE IS ON THE VERGE OF COLLAPSE?!
THAT'S RIGHT... THE SORCERY THAT SHORES UP THE CASTLE'S FOUNDATION HAS BEEN DECAYING OVER THE YEARS AND HAS ALMOST COMPLETELY FADED AWAY!

MY GUESS IS THE CASTLE WILL HOLD UP FOR ANOTHER THREE DAYS TOPS.
Ba-bye!
YOU SHOULD HAVE TOLD ME ABOUT THIS EARLIER!!
THE DEMON CASTLE WAS BUILT...
...BY THE PREVIOUS DEMON KING LORD MIDNIGHT. IT CAN ONLY BE SUSTAINED BY LORD MIDNIGHT'S SORCERY!
I CAN'T BELIEVE IT... WHY DOES HADES ALWAYS WAIT UNTIL THE LAST MINUTE TO ASK ME FOR HELP?!
...

NOW I HAVE TO GO SEE FATHER ... ARGH!
HYUUUUU
AND IF YOU ANNOY HIM IN ANY WAY...
...BOTH THE DEMON CASTLE AND THE OLD DEMON CASTLE COULD GET BLOWN TO SMITHEREENS...
TELL ME SOMETHING I DON'T KNOW ...

126th Night: Longing for a Life on Demon Easy Street♡

WHAT CHOICE DO I HAVE...?
I HAVE TO VISIT MY FATHER, THE FORMER DEMON KING MIDNIGHT...
...IN THE SEALED REALM OF PANDE-MONIUM WHERE HE WENT TO RETIRE.

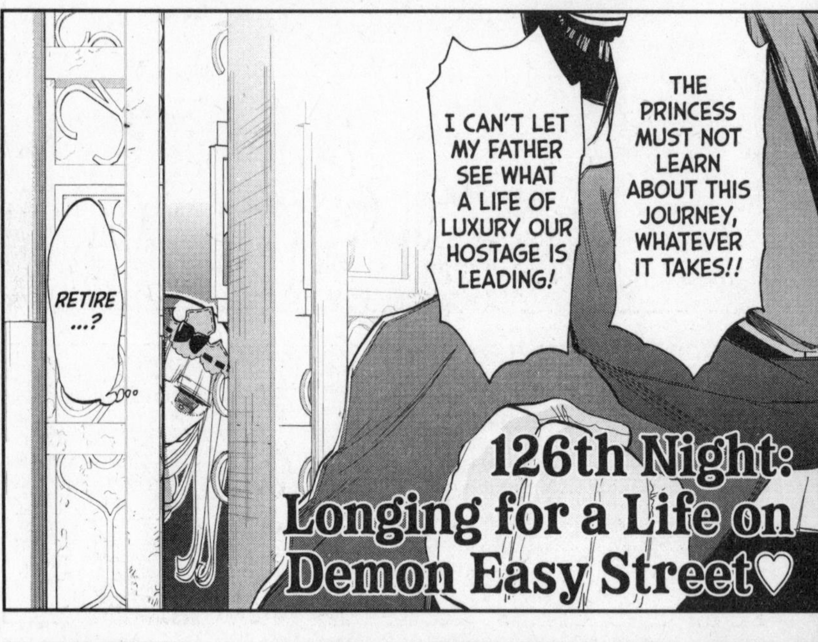
THE PRINCESS MUST NOT LEARN ABOUT THIS JOURNEY, WHATEVER IT TAKES!!
I CAN'T LET MY FATHER SEE WHAT A LIFE OF LUXURY OUR HOSTAGE IS LEADING!
RETIRE...?

126th Night: Longing for a Life on Demon Easy Street♡

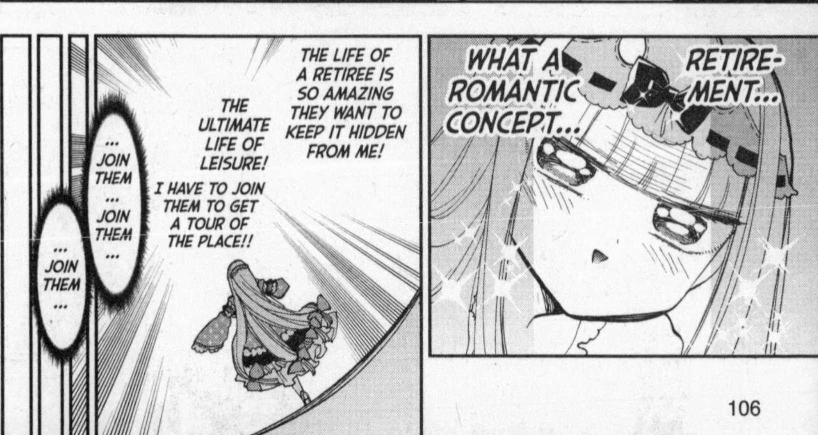
RETIRE-MENT...
WHAT A ROMANTIC CONCEPT...
THE LIFE OF A RETIREE IS SO AMAZING THEY WANT TO KEEP IT HIDDEN FROM ME!
THE ULTIMATE LIFE OF LEISURE!
I HAVE TO JOIN THEM TO GET A TOUR OF THE PLACE!!
...JOIN THEM ...JOIN THEM ...
...JOIN THEM ...

The next day...
PAN
DEMON
IUM
...
...
TMP
SHE'S HERE!!
I EXPLORED EVERY AVENUE TO GATHER INTEL ON THIS PLACE...
...BECAUSE SOMEDAY WHEN I RETIRE, I WANT MY DAYS TO BE FULL OF FUN AND NAPS TOO!
THEY AL-READY ARE!

WAIT! THIS MAKES NO SENSE! WE MADE SURE TO HIDE EVEN THE DATE OF OUR VISIT FROM HER!
SHOW ME THE SURVEILLANCE FOOTAGE FROM THE CASTLE CCTV... STARTING FROM THE MOMENT WE DECIDED TO COME HERE!
YES SIR!
VIIIP
WE'LL DEPART TOMOR-ROW... AT THE CRACK OF DAWN.
WHERE IN THE WORLD WERE YOU EAVES-DROPPING ON US FROM?
I DON'T SEE YOU...

...ANY-WHERE!
Now do you see?
EEEEEK!!

I'M SCARED! THAT WAS CREEPY!
HUH?! HOW DID YOU MANAGE TO GET INTO THAT STRANGE POSITION?!

LIKE THIS.
TA DAH
THAT IS NO POSITION FOR A PRIN-CESS!

AND WHAT'S WITH THE WEIRD LOOK ON YOUR FACE?
HUH...?

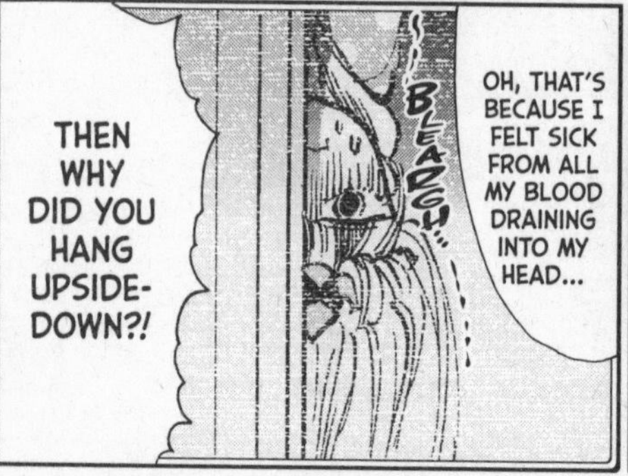
OH, THAT'S BECAUSE I FELT SICK FROM ALL MY BLOOD DRAINING INTO MY HEAD...
BLEARGH...
THEN WHY DID YOU HANG UPSIDE-DOWN?!

THIS STILL MAKES NO SENSE. THE TIME AND DATE WE DISCUSSED THAT DAY WAS FALSE.
WE TOLD EACH OTHER THE **REAL** SCHEDULE LATER.
THE ACTUAL DEPARTURE TIME WILL BE EARLY MORNING, THE DAY AFTER TOMORROW.
GOTCHA.
HUH...?

Now do you see?
EEEEEEEK!!

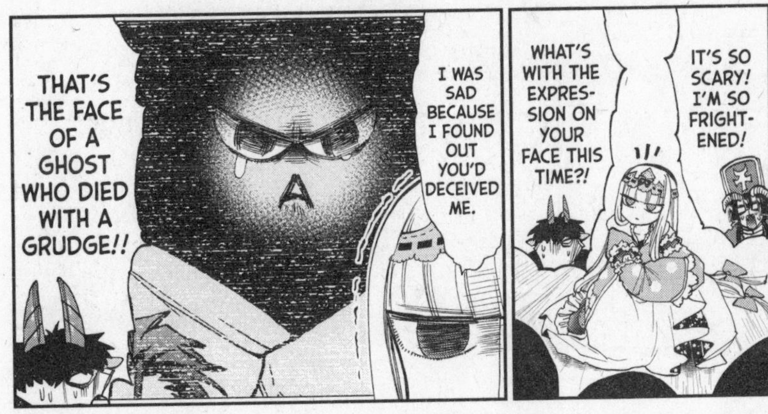
IT'S SO SCARY! I'M SO FRIGHT-ENED!
WHAT'S WITH THE EXPRES-SION ON YOUR FACE THIS TIME?!
I WAS SAD BECAUSE I FOUND OUT YOU'D DECEIVED ME.
THAT'S THE FACE OF A GHOST WHO DIED WITH A GRUDGE!!

WAIT, WAIT! I STILL DON'T GET IT! HOW DID YOU FIND OUT WHERE WE WERE MEETING?!
I'M 100 PERCENT SURE THERE WAS NO ONE AROUND WHEN WE DISCUSSED IT.
BIP
BIP
SEE ...?
YOU'RE NO-WHERE TO BE ...

Now do you see?
WHAT ARE YOU, A NINJA ?!

THIS IS A WATER-RELEASE NINJA ART...
WHAT ARE YOU, A NINJA ?! (REPEATING)
?
HUH...? BUT THAT WASN'T SCARY, WAS IT?
THAT'S NOT THE POINT!

WHAT ...? ARE YOU SAYING YOU WERE THERE THEN TOO?
B/D

...
...
STAAARE

OH! BEHIND THE WALL!!
PEEL
BINGO!

AND THE NEXT TIME ...?
...
...

AHA! THE SUIT OF ARMOR BEHIND US!
BINGO!

HURRAY!
THIS ISN'T A QUIZ SHOW!!
SORRY!!

LIS-TEN UP!
IT'S A SERIOUS PROBLEM THAT THE PRINCESS ROAMS THE CASTLE AS SHE PLEASES. THAT'S ON ME.
BUT THE BIGGER PROBLEM IS THAT NONE OF YOU NOTICED HER ALL THOSE TIMES! SHE'S HUMAN! ON TOP OF THAT, SHE'S A PRINCESS!
BIP

RMBL RMBL RMBL RMBL RMBL
COULD IT BE THAT SHE'S ALSO A NINJA ...?

A-ANYWAY! WE CAN'T LET HER OUTSMART US AGAIN!
SHE ISN'T THAT POWER-FUL PHYSI-CALLY, AFTER ALL...
VIIP

Tomorrow...
Memo
Memo
Early morning...
A CHINESE ACROBAT ...?

E-EVEN IF THE PRIN-CESS DID BUST OUT A BUNCH OF WEIRD ACROBATIC MOVES...
...HOW DID SHE MANAGE TO SNEAK AROUND BEHIND OUR BACKS WITHOUT ANY OF US NOTICING HER?
SHHFF

EVER SINCE I CAME TO THE DEMON CASTLE ...
...I'VE BEEN GETTING A LOT OF PRACTICE MOVING NOISE-LESSLY.
ACK!
THAT'S THE SKILLSET OF AN ASSAS-SIN!!
SH-SHE'S BEEN TEMPERED IN BATTLE ...

A-ANY-WAY ...
THE UP-SHOT IS, I CANNOT ALLOW YOU TO MEET MY FATHER, PRINCESS!
TH-THAT'S RIGHT! IF HE FINDS OUT YOU'RE OUR HOSTAGE, HE'LL... HE'LL...
... HE'LL ...

HE'LL GET SUPER MAD AT ALL OF YOU.
IF YOU ALREADY KNEW THAT, WHY DID YOU FOL-LOW US HERE?!

DON'T WORRY, I PROMISE I'LL BEHAVE.
TUP TUP
I WORKED SO HARD TO GATHER THIS INTEL THAT I'M VERYYY SLEEPY NOW...
Unbelievable...
I'LL MEET THE DEMON KING'S RETIRED FATHER AFTER A LITTLE NAP.
fwmp
ZZZZ...

...
...
HUH?
CAN'T WE SEIZE THIS OPPORTUNITY TO TOSS HER OUTSIDE?
Oh!
UM... NOPE. SORRY. I'VE ALREADY SEALED THE GATE, AND IT TAKES THREE HOURS TO UNSEAL IT.
W-WELL, IF WE LEAVE HER HERE, AT LEAST SHE WON'T MEET LORD MIDNIGHT...

HISSSSSSS!
Midnight's pets
GRRRRRRR!
CHOMP

SHE IS SUCH A PAIN!!
TP TP TP TP
TPTPTPTP

DID I FAIL?!
DO YOU THINK I KIDNAPPED THE WRONG PRINCESS?!
W-WELL...

IT'S NOT THAT YOU'VE FAILED, MY LIEGE... BUT RATHER THAT SHE IS A FAILURE AS A PRINCESS...
TP TPTP TPTPTP
DO YOU THINK FATHER WILL FORGIVE ME IF I TELL HIM THAT?
PROBABLY NOT.
Next chapter, meet Daddy!

Pandemonium Corridor:
An Alternate Dimension Walkway

Ominousness: ☆☆☆☆☆☆☆☆
Tranquilness: ☆☆☆☆☆☆☆☆☆

The one who bit Syalis is named Piranha.

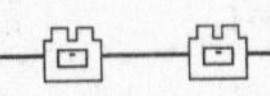

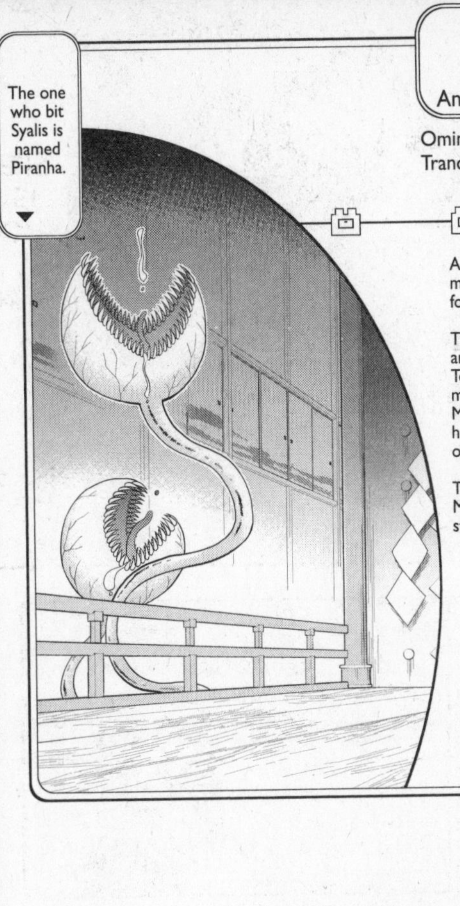

A corridor leading to Pandemonium's main edifice, the residence of retired former Demon King Midnight.

There are numerous entrances, both big and small, to this alternate dimension. To enter it, a member of demon royalty must remove the seal. Not only that, Midnight's pets, Piranha and Plant, won't hesitate to bite you, so the difficulty level of this zone is quite high.

The entire place was built to Midnight's specifications. It bears a strong resemblance to Hell Kusatsu.

Problem ten years ago:
"This place has turned into a catio and dog run for my pets."

Current problem:
"I shouldn't have made the procedures for entering this area so complicated."

THE SKILL OF WALKING NOISE-LESSLY...
THE SKILL OF LURKING UNDER-WATER...
THE SKILL OF CLINGING TO THE WALL...
I LEARNED THEM ALL FROM THE GHOST SHROUDS!
WOW!

Would you like to change your class?
3 changes remaining
▶Yes
No
Superhero
"I will gather everyone's sleepiness in my fist!"

Story thus far...
The Demon King and his entourage have come to meet with the retired former Demon King Midnight to ask him to restore the crumbling structure of the Old Demon Castle.
I want a retire-ment tour!
Together with the princess, who followed them, they reluctantly venture deeper into Pandemonium...

THE PRINCESS IS STILL ASLEEP.
WHAT ARE WE GONNA DO...? IF WE KEEP GOING, LORD MIDNIGHT IS GOING TO FIND OUT HOW LITTLE CON-TROL WE HAVE OVER OUR HOSTAGE!
HEE HEE HEE HEE HEE
RIGHT...

WE HAVE NO CHOICE BUT TO INTRODUCE HER TO HIM AS A DEMON! THEN WE CAN PERMIT THE PRIN-CESS TO BE FREE-RANGE AS USUAL...
OP-ERATION ALIS-ALIS!
*Cute code name
LET'S GO WITH THAT PLAN.
AND NOW THE TIME HAS COME...
...FOR OUR AUDIENCE WITH THE FORMER DEMON KING LORD MIDNIGHT!

127th Night: Your Son Is a Hard Worker

127th Night: Your Son Is a Hard Worker

127th Night:
Your Son Is a Hard Worker
YOU MAY ENTER ...

AH, MY SON TWILIGHT!
Former Demon King Midnight

IT'S G-GOOD TO SEE YOU, FATHER. IT'S BEEN TOO LONG.
HAVE YOU BEEN WELL?
YES!
HE'S EVEN BIGGER THAN BEFORE... WHAT AN IMPOSING PRESENCE!
YES, I'M VERY GLAD HE'S ON OUR SIDE.
...
WE HAVE TO HIDE THE HOSTAGE FROM HIM NO MATTER WHAT!

AND WHO... IS THAT?
SHDDDR

OH! UM...
A D-DEMON! A NEW GUARDIAN...
I SEE ...

...
WE PULLED IT OFF!!
WHO CARES IF HE THINKS SHE'S A LITTLE ODD?
WE ONLY NEED TO CONCEAL THAT THE HOSTAGE FOLLOWED US IN HERE.

SO, F-FATHER... THE REASON FOR MY VISIT TODAY IS...
blink
She woke up.
...
She's thinking, "So **that's** the Demon King's father! He sure is big!"
...
...!
She's thinking, "Oh, that's right! I promised to...
...behave in his presence!"

WHY IS SHE... PLACING HAND-CUFFS... ON HER-SELF?

AIIIEEEEE!!
*The princess's concept of proper hostage attire
H-HOS-TAGE STYLE?!
WHY IS SHE PUT-TING THOSE ON NOW OF ALL TIMES?!
UM, TH-THAT'S BE-CAUSE...
SHE LOOKS LIKE A HOSTAGE.
OR SOME KIND OF CAP-TIVE.

OH N-NO!!
PRINCESS! PLEASE ACT NORMAL NOW! PLEASE!
!

ANYWAY, F-FATHER, I CAME TO ASK YOU FOR A FAVOR TODAY, AND–
?

KLING KLING KLING
KLING KLING KLING
FOR DOGS
Doggie door
Midnight's bedroom

AIIIEEEEE!
The princess's idea of normal.
WHAT ... ARE YOU ... DOING?
HUH?
I'M BREAKING THE LOCK TO ESCAPE LIKE I ALWAYS DO, OF COURSE.
...

YOU'RE ALWAYS ESCAPING ...?

FOR DOGS
UH-HUH. BECAUSE I'M ALWAYS LOCKED IN MY ROOM.

ALWAYS LOCKED IN...?
NOOOOOO!!

IT'S AS IF SHE'S...
WHAT?! OH NO, NO, NO! SH-SHE'S A COMPLETELY ORDINARY DEMON!
HE'S GETTING WARMER, BUT HE HASN'T FIGURED IT OUT YET! I MUST HELP MY LIEGE OUT SOMEHOW!

THIS IS SO COMFY... JUST LIKE MY USUAL CELL...
She's starting to feel at home in cell-like rooms.
STOOOOOP!
HER USUAL CELL ...?
HE'S GETTING MORE SUSPI-CIOUS!

UM, P-PLEASE DON'T GIVE HER A SECOND THOUGHT!
SHE EALLY S JUST N OR-DINARY EMON WHO–
IS THIS A CUSHION ...?
DRAG DRAG
IT'S JUST LIKE MY BED BACK IN MY HOME CASTLE ...
FOR DOGS

...
HER... HOME CASTLE ...?
IS SHE... SOME SORT OF...
... ROYALTY ?
HE'S GETTING WAAAARM-ER!!

WHAT ARE WE GOING TO DO?! AT THIS RATE, HE'LL FIGURE IT OUT ANY MINUTE NOW!
WE NEED TO LEAVE ASAP!
HURRY UP AND ASK HIM TO RESTORE THE OLD DEMON CASTLE!

OKAY, OKAY!
UM... FATHER! WE CAME HERE...
...TODAY TO ASK YOU FOR AN IMPORTANT FAVOR...

FATHER ...?
Just at that moment ... ... Midnight is thinking ...

THIS YOUNG WOMAN... WHO IS SHE, REALLY?

IF SHE WERE JUST AN ORDINARY ROOKIE DEMON, WHY WOULD THEY BOTHER INTRODUCING HER TO ME?
THAT WOULDN'T MAKE ANY SENSE!

AT FIRST I THOUGHT SHE MIGHT ACTUALLY BE HUMAN, BUT...

STK STK

...NOT ONLY IS SHE UNAFRAID OF ME...
...SHE'S EVEN WRITING HER NAME ON MY CUSHION!
NO ONE OF SOUND MIND WOULD DO THAT...
...LET ALONE A HUMAN.
*Human

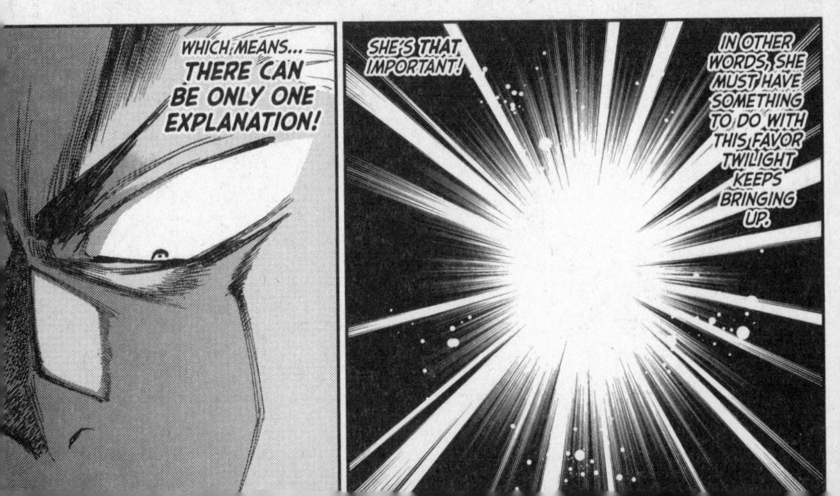
IN OTHER WORDS, SHE MUST HAVE SOMETHING TO DO WITH THIS FAVOR TWILIGHT KEEPS BRINGING UP.
SHE'S THAT IMPORTANT!
WHICH MEANS... THERE CAN BE ONLY ONE EXPLANATION!

THIS YOUNG WOMAN MUST BE...
...TWILIGHT'S WIFE!!

UM, FATHER? ER...
I KNOW...
WHAT YOU HAVE COME TO ASK ME...
FATHER?!
YOU DO?! GREAT, THEN YOU'LL-
THAT'S RIGHT. BUT...

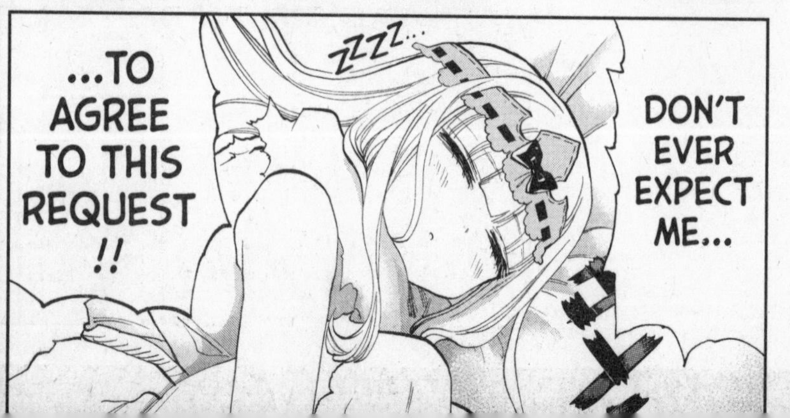
ZZZZ...
DON'T EVER EXPECT ME...
...TO AGREE TO THIS REQUEST!!

Pandemonium's Main Edifice

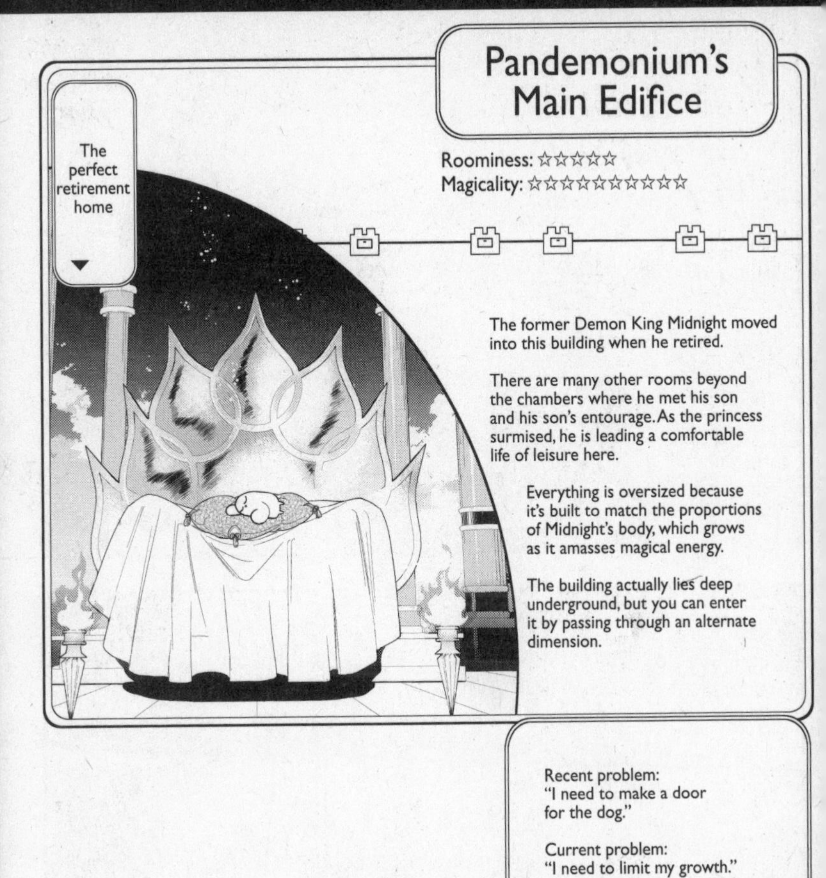

The perfect retirement home

Roominess: ☆☆☆☆☆
Magicality: ☆☆☆☆☆☆☆☆☆☆☆☆

The former Demon King Midnight moved into this building when he retired.

There are many other rooms beyond the chambers where he met his son and his son's entourage. As the princess surmised, he is leading a comfortable life of leisure here.

Everything is oversized because it's built to match the proportions of Midnight's body, which grows as it amasses magical energy.

The building actually lies deep underground, but you can enter it by passing through an alternate dimension.

Recent problem:
"I need to make a door for the dog."

Current problem:
"I need to limit my growth."

THIS IS SO COMFY... JUST LIKE MY USUAL CELL...
...
Oh?
...
What's wrong?
Even the princess realizes it's odd for her to be fond of her cell.
(But she brushes the thought off.)

Would you like to change your class?
2 changes remaining
▶Yes
No
Hostage
"A meek and well-behaved appearance."

128th Night: Daddy Is a Worrywart

The Demon King is visiting his retired father Midnight to ask him to repair the Old Demon Castle, which is on the verge of collapse.

The demons have been doing their best to hide the identity of the princess, who followed them there, from Midnight.

Now the situation has turned into...

...a terrible case of mistaken identity.
THIS YOUNG WOMAN MUST BE...
...TWI-LIGHT'S WIFE!!
Wrong.

I SEE! THIS DELEGATION HAS COME TO ASK ME TO ACCEPT THEIR MARRIAGE UNION!
Wrong.

DON'T EVER EXPECT ME TO AGREE TO THIS RE-QUEST!!

IT'S 500 YEARS TOO SOON FOR YOU!
YOU, YOU...
...CAL-LOW YOUTH!!
F-FOR SOME REASON...
...HE'S REALLY MAD AT ME!!

128th Night: Daddy Is a Worrywart

BUT WHAT IS HE MAD ABOUT...?!
ALL WE WERE GOING TO ASK WAS IF HE WOULD COME AND REPAIR THE OLD DEMON CASTLE!
WE MAN-AGED TO SUCCESS-FULLY HIDE THE PRINCESS'S IDENTITY.
OR DID WE...? MAYBE HE'S SEEN THROUGH OUR PRE-TENSE...
?!

I THINK HE FIG-URED OUT THAT THE PRINCESS IS ACTU-ALLY OUR HOSTAGE ...
...AND HE'S MAD AT YOU FOR TURNING TO YOUR FATHER FOR HELP WHEN YOU'RE THE REIGNING DEMON KING.
!
IS FATHER SCOLDING ME BECAUSE HE'S SEEN THROUGH OUR RUSE?!
IS THIS BECAUSE... HE CARES ABOUT ME?
Actually, at that very moment, Midnight is thinking...

DID I RAISE HIM WRONG?
IF WHAT TWILIGHT'S WIFE (PENDING MY APPROVAL) WAS SAYING IS TRUE...
... THEN MY SON IS A SCUM-BAG WHO BEATS HIS WOMAN!
IT CAN'T BE... I'D BETTER DOUBLE-CHECK WITH HER!

WOMAN ...

YOU WERE TALKING ABOUT YOUR LIFE JUST A MOMENT AGO... TELL ME MORE ABOUT HOW YOU SPEND YOUR DAYS.
...

THEY MAKE ME... STAY INSIDE MY CELL...
Midnight Vision
Reality
BAM
HEY! QUIT BREAKING OUT!

OH!
I DO WHAT I MUST!

YOU DON'T HAVE WHAT IT TAKES FOR THIS!
?!
W-WHAT ?!

TELL ME MORE, WOMAN...
HUH?

WELL, I TOLD THEM I WANTED TO GO HOME, AND THEY YELLED AT ME...
Midnight Vision
Ohh... Ohh...
I long for home...
Reality
I want to go home to get my wool undies...
Fdgt
Fdgt
BAD!

UM... I'M VERY STRICT WITH HER!
Midnight Vision
I want to see my fami-lyyyy!
Reality
LOSS PREVENTION

I COMMEND YOU FOR... YOUR WICKEDNESS ...
HUH?!
WHAT ELSE, WOMAN ...?
WHAT ELSE?
fluffy fluffy

UM... OH, I DIE AT LEAST ONCE A WEEK!
Midnight Vision
I'd rather die!
Reality
SPLASH
Tee hee
PRINCEEESS!

OH, DON'T WORRY, FATHER! WE ALWAYS BRING HER BACK TO LIFE!
YES! I TAKE CARE OF THAT!
Midnight Vision
Even death is no escape for me ...
Reality
Hey! I slept soooo well.

...
TWILIGHT ...

SHFFF
YOU IMPRISON HER (YOUR WIFE) IN A CELL...
YOU DON'T PERMIT HER TO VISIT HER HOME... AND YOU CONTROL HER EVERY MOVE. HAVE I GOT THAT RIGHT?
HUH ...?

ISN'T THAT THE PROPER WAY TO TREAT A HOSTAGE?
HE WOULD NEVER CALL YOU A CALLOW YOUTH IF YOU COULD ACTUALLY PULL ALL THAT OFF!
THERE SEEMS TO BE A MISUNDER-STANDING... THOSE ARE THE BASIC TENETS OF HOSTAGE CARE AND MAINTE-NANCE.
...

OF COURSE! THAT'S RIGHT!

I DIDN'T RAISE YOU TO BEHAVE LIKE THIS!
VEEEE
W-W-WHAT?!

ARRRRGH?!?!?!
WHUDDD
VEEEE

YOU'RE WORSE THAN A CALLOW YOUTH! DOES THE BLOOD IN YOUR VEINS RUN COLD?!
WHERE DID I GO WRONG, MY BELOVED SON?!
F-FA-THER?!
KRABOOM
KRANCH
I WILL NOT ALLOW THIS!
FA-THER?!
RMBL RMBL RMBL RMBL RMBL
KRASH
Peaceful princess

AS I SUS-PECTED, HE'S CLEARLY ...
... MISTAKEN ABOUT SOMETHING ...

BUT WHAT COULD IT BE ...?
HOW COULD YOU?!
THAT IS NO WAY TO TREAT ...
... YOUR WIFE !!

...
M-MY... WIFE ?!
WHAT DO YOU HAVE TO SAY FOR YOURSELF?
SHE IS YOUR WIFE, ISN'T SHE?

WHAT?!
FA SH

KRAKKABOOOM

HISSSS...
WHAT?! YOU ONLY CAME HERE TO ASK ME TO REPAIR THE OLD DEMON CASTLE?!
THAT'S RIGHT ...

I MISUNDERSTOOD. MY APOLOGIES.
BUT IN THAT CASE... IF SHE'S NOT YOUR WIFE...
...WHO IS THAT YOUNG WOMAN?
UM ...

...
HE'S GOING TO CHEW ME OUT WHEN I FESS UP...
UM... ACTUALLY...
SHE'S OUR HUMAN HOSTAGE.

OH, I SEE.
HE'S SO MELLOW ABOUT IT!

HUH?! UM, FATHER... AREN'T YOU GOING TO SCOLD ME ABOUT THE HOSTAGE?
HRM.... IT'S UNFORTUNATE THAT SHE'S SO FREE-SPIRITED, BUT...I HAVE NO INTENTION OF MEDDLING IN YOUR BUSINESS.
BESIDES ...

Cookie
...SHE'S HITTING IT OFF WELL WITH COOKIE. SO I'LL ALLOW YOU TO CARRY ON AS YOU ARE.
LORD MIDNIGHT, I THINK YOU'VE MELLOWED OUT A BIT TOO MUCH SINCE YOU RETIRED.

NNNNN...
ANY-WAY...
...IT'S HARD TO BELIEVE THAT A HUMAN COULD SLEEP SO PEACEFULLY IN THE DEMON REALM.

OH, AND, UM... ABOUT THE OLD DEMON CASTLE ...?
LET'S GO FIX IT AFTER SHE WAKES UP.
HE'S SO MELLOW ABOUT THAT TOO!
HIS NAME IS COOKIE?!
LIKE FATHER, LIKE SON ...
The princess decides to get a dog when she retires.

A Shetland sheepdog

Cookie

Upon his retirement, the former Demon King Midnight got himself a dog. Cookie is three years old.

He was only an ordinary quadrupedal dog at first, but he transformed into this bestial hound under the influence of Midnight's power.

Since Cookie's master is so large, he treats Cookie more like a bunny than a dog.

Cookie's impression when meeting Great Red Siberian, a fellow bestial hound, was that Red's face is scary.

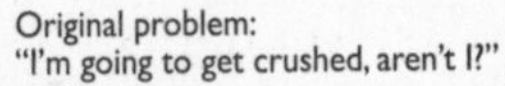

Original problem:
"I'm going to get crushed, aren't I?"

Current problem:
"I long to herd sheep."

Upon first meeting, they both sensed that the other was burdened with cares.

...
...

Would you like to change your class?
1 change remaining
▶Yes
No
Beekeeper
"Arrgh! I hate bees! Arrgh."

129th Night: Demon Castle: Dad and Me and Sometimes the Hostage

After repairing the Old Demon Castle...
...Midnight decided to visit Twilight's Demon Castle.
YOU'RE GOING TO DROP BY?!

TROMP
TROMP
UH-HUH. I MIGHT AS WELL DROP BY WHILE I'M IN THE NEIGHBOR-HOOD.
!
THIS IS A GREAT OPPOR-TUNITY!
THE PERFECT CHANCE TO SHOW OFF!

I'LL G-GIVE YOU A PERSONAL TOUR OF THE CASTLE!
PLUS, I'LL GET TO SPEND QUAL-ITY TIME WITH FATHER.
IT'S BEEN A LONG TIME SINCE WE'VE SEEN EACH OTHER. I'LL IMPRESS HIM WITH ALL MY ACCOMPLISH-MENTS!

FATHER!
OVER HERE!

129th Night: Demon Castle: Dad and Me and Sometimes the Hostage

Whee
Whee
Whee

Whee Whee
*Work hours

Whee
TWI-LIGHT ...?
Whee
Whee
Whee
YES ...?
...

UM... THE H-HORNS ...
Whee
Whee
I'D LIKE TO POINT OUT THE NEW HORNS...
...ATOP THE DEMON CASTLE ...

Whee
Whee
...
...

...
THEY SEEM TO BE DIGGING HOLES IN THEM...
MAINTE-NANCE!
IT'S ONLY THE DAILY MAINTE-NANCE!

...
...

THE MAINTE-NANCE IS DONE BY... THE HOS-TAGE?
AIIIEEEEE!!

SH-SHOOT! MOVING ON... LET'S MOVE ON!
U-UM... LOOK OVER HERE!
Ooh.
Ooh.

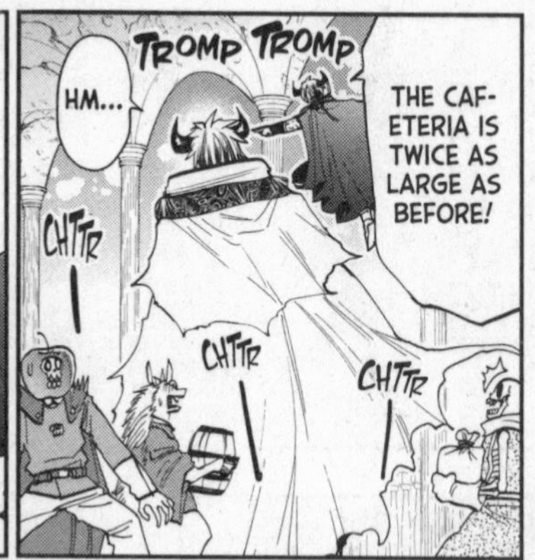
TROMP TROMP
THE CAF-ETERIA IS TWICE AS LARGE AS BEFORE!
HM...
CHTTR
CHTTR
CHTTR

DEMON CASTLE CAFET
HOW DO YOU LIKE IT?!
THE INTERIOR DESIGN REMODEL IS VERY SOPHIS-TICA...

FLOPP
*Work hours

TWILI-
UM ...
...

A MEETING!
THEY'RE HAVING A BUSINESS MEETING!
THAT'S A SUNKEN KOTATSU—THERE'S A LOT OF ROOM INSIDE!
HM...

...
I SEE ...
LET'S PLAY SHIRITORI! I'LL START WITH... SHIRITORI. IT ENDS WITH AN I...
INK. ENDS WITH A K.
IDIOOOOOOOTS!

TWI-LIGHT ...?
Ka-buki.
Ink.
Ka-buki.
TWO STRIKES ...

ARGH! HE'S IR-RITATED! I CAN'T LET THAT HAPPEN AGAIN!
N-NEXT UP...
IT'S NO USE! I HAVE A TERRIBLE PREMONITION I'M GOING TO STRIKE OUT NO MAT-TER WHERE I TAKE HIM.
WAVER
WAVER
THE ONLY ONE...

...I CAN TRUST...
...IS MYSELF !!
TROMP
TROMP
W-WHY DON'T YOU TAKE A LOOK AT MY ROOM NEXT?

IT'LL BE FINE ...
RRRMMMBL RRRMMMBL
IT'LL BE FINE ...
THIS IS MY BED-ROOM ...
RRR RM MM BLLL

BAM
OH GOOD, YOU'RE HERE!
WE PROMISED TO PLAY PILLOW FIGHT (HARD MODE) TODAY, REMEMBER?
PILLOW FIGHT

OHHH
THREE STRIKES, I'M OUT!!

TWI-LIGHT...
UM... I H-HAVE NO IDEA WHAT SHE'S TALKING ABOUT!
I TOTALLY FORGOT! I'M SUCH AN IDIOT!
TODAY WE'RE ALLOWED TO PUT ROCKS IN OUR PILLOWS...
...BUT WE'RE ALSO ALLOWED TO USE SHIELDS TO PROTECT OURSELVES, RIGHT?!
THAT'S RIGHT, BUT... PLEASE STOP!!

I'M DONE FOR! FATHER'S RAGE...
...IS COMING TO A BOIL!
I'M SPEECHLESS...

!

I HAD NO INTENTION OF CRITIQUING THE JOB YOU'RE DOING...
...BUT THIS IS BEYOND MY WILDEST IMAGIN-INGS!

I ALWAYS THOUGHT YOU LACKED DIGNITY.
OH...

HE CAN'T EVEN BE BOTHERED TO SCOLD ME ANY-MORE.
HE'S COMPLETELY GIVEN UP ON ME.

YOU'RE ENTIRELY RESPONSIBLE FOR THE STATE OF THIS CASTLE...
Should I wait?

I- I'M S-SORR...

EVERYONE IN THE CASTLE IS SO ENERGIZED AND OPTIMISTIC!
THEY'RE ALL SMILING EVEN THOUGH WE'RE IN THE MIDST OF A WAR AGAINST THE HUMANS.
!

THIS IS A FAR CRY FROM THE MOOD DURING MY REIGN...
F-FATHER?!

B-BUT, FATHER! I'M... NOT LIKE YOU...

YOU SHOULD HAVE MORE CONFIDENCE. YOU'VE ACCOMPLISHED THINGS I WASN'T ABLE TO.

AND YOUR HOSTAGE CAN HAVE THE RUN OF THE PLACE BECAUSE OF THE ATMOSPHERE YOU'VE CREATED IN THE CASTLE.
I'M PLEASANTLY SURPRISED!

LOOK AT...
...HER FACE. HER EXPRESSION REFLECTS THE SORT OF KING YOU ARE.
PILLOW FIGHT

Pillow... fight...

THOSE ARE MY OBSERVATIONS, FOR WHAT THEY'RE WORTH.
FATHER!!
TWITCH
And so...

...the Old Demon Castle is restored, the retired former Demon King heads home and...
WHATEVER YOU'RE DOING HERE IS WORKING...

I'D STILL LIKE TO HAVE A LITTLE MORE DIGNITY THOUGH.
I'll work on that...
...the current Demon King develops a little more self-esteem.
Zzzz...

Former Demon King Midnight

Big Daddy

Dignity: ☆☆☆☆☆☆☆☆☆☆☆
Imposingness: ☆☆☆☆☆☆☆☆☆☆☆

The father of the current Demon King Twilight and a great leader of demonkind until a decade ago. He is currently retired and recovering from the fatigue induced by his long reign.

The demons and divinity species were on the verge of extinction 400 years ago. Midnight saved them by creating a home for them underground.

In those days, the Demon Castle was located beneath the surface, but when Twilight succeeded him as king, he raised the castle aboveground. (That's the current Old Demon Castle.)

Problem of a few hundred years ago: "My days are filled with nothing but battles."

Problem of a few decades ago: "He looks just like me, so why is he so darn cute?!"

TROMP
TROMP

TWI-LIGHT...
YOU COULD HAVE RAISED THE CEILING IN THE DEMON CASTLE A BIT HIGHER...
He bumped his head on it.

Would you like to change your class?
0 changes remaining

Color Gang

"Team Alisalis in da castle!"

130th Night: I Want You by My Side
The other day, Princess Syalis got a glimpse into the daily life of the retired former Demon King.

She was impressed.
HE HAS A LOT OF FREE TIME!
I THINK I CAN MIMIC HIS LIFE-STYLE...

...EXCEPT THAT I'M LACKING SOME-THING...

A...
...personal assistant!
!

HEY! COULD YOU GET ME A PERSONAL SERVANT?
PRINCESS, ARE YOU AWARE OF YOUR POSITION IN THIS CASTLE?!
Hostage
130th Night:
I Want You by My Side

GRRR
...

THAT DIDN'T WORK OUT VERY WELL. BUT I'M NOT GIVING UP YET!
A DEVOTED SERVANT DEDICATED TO SUPPORTING MY LIFESTYLE— UNLIKE THE ONES I HAD BACK HOME... HOW PLEASANT WOULD THAT BE?!
I GUESS I'LL JUST HAVE TO...
SHFF
...TRAIN THE TEDDY DEMONS TO BE MY RIGHT-HAND BEARS.

GRWR!
GRWRRR!
...

GRWR!
FLOFFP

OR NOT.
I GUESS I'M GOING TO HAVE TO SEEK OUT THE STAFF I NEED...
SLAM
Fail

...AND APPARENTLY WE'RE SHORT ON APPLICANTS THESE DAYS.
A LOT OF THE NEW CASTLE HIRES HAD TO BE HEAD-HUNTED FROM OTHER PLACES.
FOR REAL?!

I WANT TO BE HEAD-HUNTED!

CONGRATULATIONS...
CONGRATULATIONS...
KLAP... KLAP... KLAP...
?!

Business cards are a must for head-hunters!
I'M THE HOSTAGE, PRINCESS AURORA SYA LIS GOODE-RESTE.
?!
I KNOW THAT!
TO TELL YOU THE TRUTH...
Oh!
IF I ASK HIM DIRECTLY TO BE MY SERVANT, I MIGHT GET IN TROUBLE AGAIN...
I'LL BE CIRCUM-SPECT AND ONLY TELL HIM ABOUT THE NA-TURE OF THE WORK FOR NOW...
...
Servant candidate A: Quilly
?

I WANT YOU TO... ALWAYS BE BY MY SIDE FROM MORNING TILL NIGHT.
*Basic duties
?!

From morning...
...till night...
Picturing

Always...
Picturing
...together...
...
...
?
HUH? MAYBE I WASN'T ENTHU-SIASTIC ENOUGH?

BAM
UM, I'M TALKING ABOUT MY FUTURE...
WH-WHAT?!
IS THIS YOUR IDEA OF A JOKE?!
QUIL-LADIL-LOOOOO!!
?!

Ahhhhh!
...?

WHAT WAS THAT ALL ABOUT? ANYWHO, I GUESS THAT'S SETTLED!
THERE ARE FIVE DAYS IN THE WEEK, SO I'LL NEED FOUR MORE...
Tup Tup
? ?
ALL RIGHTIE ...

I'LL USE THE SAME STRATEGY.
I WANT YOU TO WATCH OVER ME ALL DAY LONG...
*Basic duties
WHAAAAAT?!
...AND SHARE MY ROOM AND BOARD.
*Pay nego-tiable
KOFF KOFF! SHOULDN'T WE TAKE THINGS ONE STEP AT A TIME...? KOFF KOFF KOFF!

The princess continues her head-hunting...
STAY WITH ME!
AHHH!
PLEASE LET ME THINK IT OVER FIRST!!
TP TP TP TP TP
...
WHAT THE HELL?!
WHY ARE YOU PROPOSING MARRIAGE TO EVERYONE?!
?

OH, SORRY. YOU'RE NOT ON THE LIST.
HUH?!
Fail
I AM KIND OF SURPRISED THEY ALL AGREED RIGHT AWAY.
I HAVE MUCH MORE TO EXPLAIN TO THEM ABOUT THEIR DUTIES...
I HAVE AN IDEA...

I'LL BE EVEN CLEARER MOVING FORWARD.
DASH DASH
ACK! IS THAT THE PRINCESS?!
OH! D-DEMON CLERIC!

WHAT?
GRAB

I WANT TO BE WITH YOU FROM MORNING TILL NIGHT!
*Explaining his basic duties
?!?!

WELL?
W-WHAT...?
?!

UM... PRINCESS?
WHAT... DID YOU JUST SAY?

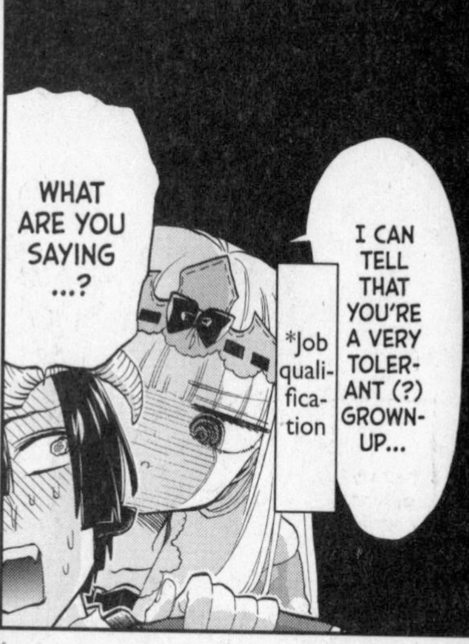
I CAN TELL THAT YOU'RE A VERY TOLERANT (?) GROWN-UP...
*Job qualification
WHAT ARE YOU SAYING ...?

DON'T WORRY, WE'LL START WITH A VERBAL AGREEMENT AND SIGN A CONTRACT LATER!
*Job offer
CONTRACT?!
ARE YOU...? PRINCESS, DO YOU MEAN ...?
AND ... UMM ...

... LOOK AFTER ME UNTIL DEATH DO US PART.
*Resurrection request
...
...
Image
KA
BOOM
DEMON CLERIIIIIC!

BYE! WE'LL START TOMORROW!
TEE HEE HEE ...
Um
urk
ack
SERVANT HEADHUNT COMPLETE!
Aiiieee
Arrgh
DEMON CLERIC HAS TURNED TO STONE!

PHEW... I'M GOOD NOW!
I'VE GOT FIVE SERVANTS TAKING TURNS ATTENDING ME ON WEEKDAYS, AND THEY'LL ALL GET WEEKENDS OFF...
I'VE EVEN TAKEN THEIR WORK-LIFE BALANCE INTO CONSIDERATION. MY PLAN IS FLAWLESS.
Notorious for dragging everyone into her quagmires

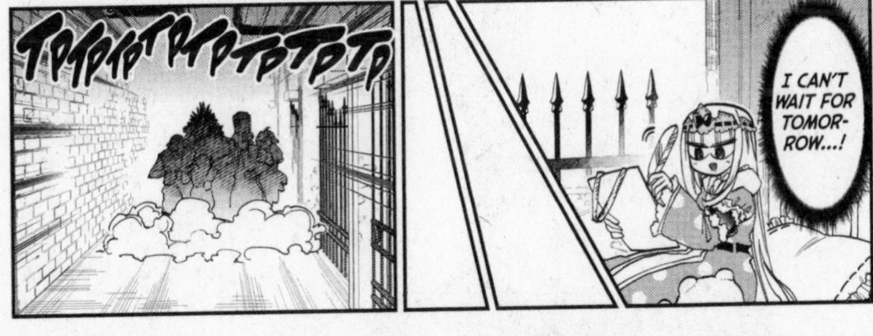
I CAN'T WAIT FOR TOMORROW...!
TPTPTPTPTPTPTPTPTPTP

PRINCESS!!
WE CANNOT ACCEPT THESE SUDDEN MARRIAGE PROPOSALS!

ZZZZ...
PERSONAL ATTENDANT ROSTER
MON
TUE
WED
THUR
FRI

I'M LOOKING FORWARD TO...
...BEING ATTENDED TO AND PAMPERED.

PERSONAL ATTENDANT ROSTER
MON
TUE
WED
THUR
FRI
...

The next day...
NO ONE'S SHOWED UP TO WORK ...
?
In the end, the princess's career as a headhunter was a dismal failure.

Before Repairing the Old Demon Castle

LORD MIDNIGHT! LONG TIME NO SEE!
OH! HELLO, HADES!
HUH ...?
WHAT ARE YOU DOING AT THE OLD DEMON CASTLE?
OH NO! WE CAN'T LET HIM FIND OUT WE'RE NOT GETTING ALONG!
Lord Midnight doesn't know that Hades ditched Twilight.
UMM.. WELL... SOMEONE HAS TO KEEP AN EYE ON THE PLACE...
FAST THINKING, HADES!
HM... I SEE... SO...
HOW ARE YOU AND TWI-LIGHT GET-TING ALONG?
B-BBMP
B-BBMP
B-BBMP
GREAT!
LIE
GRIT
WAY TO GO, HADES!
Only co-operates at times like this
Thank you very much for picking up this volume!
To be continued ...!

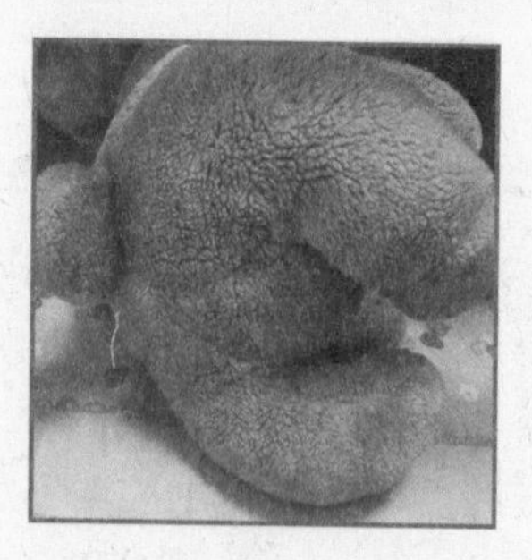

Hi, I'm Kumanomata. I've been drawing Syalis sleeping for ten volumes now!!

– KAGIJI KUMANOMATA

Grimoire Utility Travel Pillow

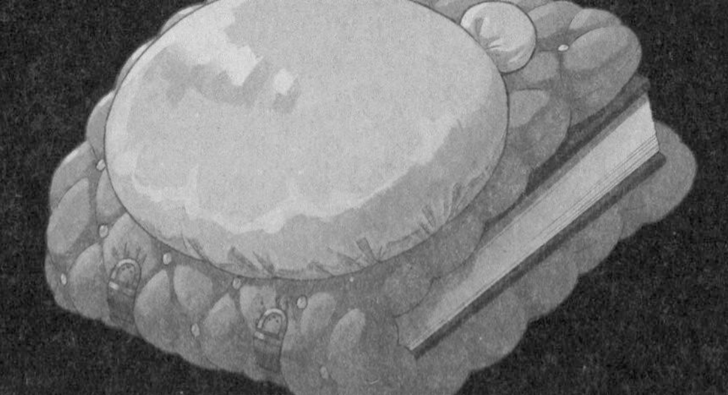

MATERIALS

Ghost Shroud

Teddy Demon Fur Stuffing

Metal Fitting from Treasure Chest

Lots of Princess Syalis's Love ▼

Teddy Demon

Princess Syalis

Alazif

Eggplant Seal

Poseidon

Cookie

Former Demon
King Midnight
Former Venom
Dragon
Demon King
Twilight
Neo Alraune
Demon Cleric
Great Red Siberian

SLEEPY PRINCESS IN THE DEMON CASTLE

10

Shonen Sunday Edition

STORY AND ART BY

KAGIJI KUMANOMATA

Original Japanese edition published by SHOGAKUKAN.
English translation rights in the United States of America, Canada, the United Kingdom, Ireland, Australia and New Zealand arranged with SHOGAKUKAN.

TRANSLATION **TETSUICHIRO MIYAKI**
ENGLISH ADAPTATION **ANNETTE ROMAN**
TOUCH-UP ART & LETTERING **JAMES GAUBATZ**
COVER & INTERIOR DESIGN **ALICE LEWIS**
EDITOR **ANNETTE ROMAN**

Printed in Canada

Published by VIZ Media, LLC
P.O. Box 77010
San Francisco, CA 94107

10 9 8 7 6 5 4 3 2 1
First printing, December 2019

ratings.viz.com
RATED
T
TEEN

PARENTAL ADVISORY
SLEEPY PRINCESS IN THE DEMON CASTLE is rated T for Teen and is recommended for ages 13 and up. This volume contains fantasy violence.

VIZ MEDIA

viz.com

SHONEN SUNDAY

shonensunday.com

VOLUME
11
Celebrate New Year's, Valentine's Day and a very special pajama party at the Demon Castle with the princess and her demon friends—er, *captors*! Then the Five Rings athletic tournament captures the imagination of demons and human alike. But when one of the athletes turns the demons' human friend—er, *hostage*—into a besotted fangirl, the castle staff doesn't take it well. Also, Syalis imbibes a potion that induces her greatest fear, Demon King Twilight desperately tries to change his image and the hero Dawner adds a certain someone to his unwelcome rescue party.